MW01079496

COLORING
INSECTOPOLIS

Dedicated to my friend,
Steve Ross, who helped
these insects crawl, hop,
and take flight.

COLORING
INSECTOPOLIS

PETER KUPER

Countryman Press

An Imprint of W. W. Norton & Company
Independent Publishers Since 1923

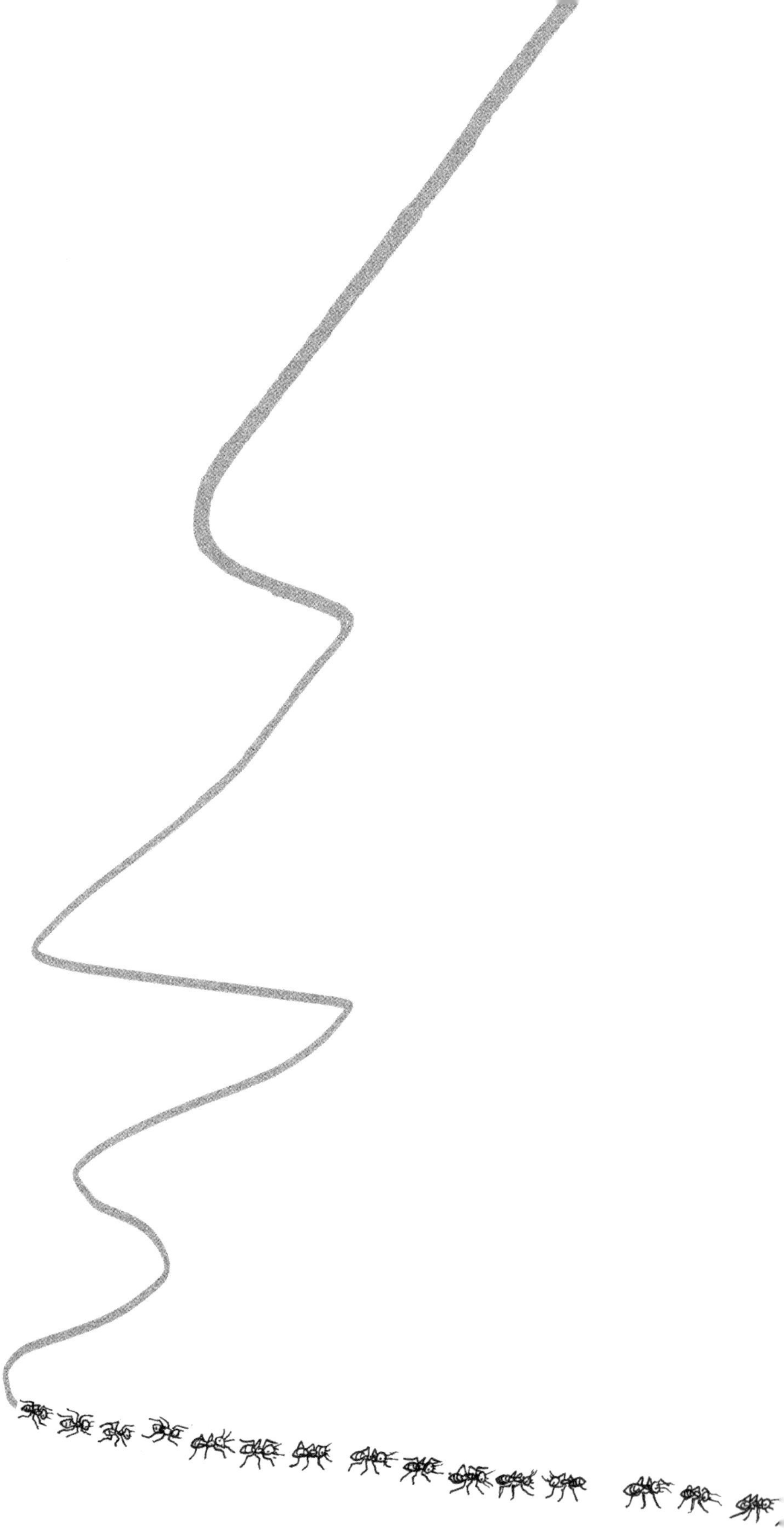

INTRODUCTION

Since I was a child, I've had a fascination with arthropods. At age four, I decided I wanted to be an entomologist—a studier of bugs. At age seven, my enthusiasm for spiders was replaced by an obsession with Spider-Man. (I know, spiders aren't insects; let's not split hairs.) Though my career path led me to cartooning, a love of insects has never left me. I concluded there must be a Venn diagram where I could pursue both interests. What you hold in your hands is an example of that diagram realized.

Coloring Insectopolis is a companion volume to my book *Insectopolis*, which began as proposed history of insects through the millennia and the people who had studied them as a graphic novel. This was the idea that won me a 2020-21 Cullman Fellowship from the New York Public Library. I was working out exactly how to tell that story and then COVID-19 hit. Although I was allowed into the library, the public was not. The hallowed institution felt like a ghost-filled, postapocalyptic environment, my steps echoing down empty halls. But on a visit to the map room to look up the flight path of the monarch butterfly, a light bulb went off in my head— I could populate the entire place with insects! (At least in my drawings.) Suddenly I had the framework for my story: People are gone and insects are thriving and studying their own history in the magnificent library. The only people to appear would be the ghosts of entomology's past, naturalists forgotten through time.

One of the things I discovered as I researched what would become the graphic novel *Insectopolis* was how similar entomologists are to comic fans. They are enthusiastic about anyone who shares their passion for insects. I found it easy to connect with some of the leading experts, all of whom were incredibly generous with their time. Through them, doors opened that allowed me to access museum collections and insured my drawings were accurate. The more I explored, the more I was able to imagine what insects might be thinking and saying to one another in their mysterious languages.

Coloring Insectopolis is your opportunity to bring life to these pen-and-ink drawings taken from *Insectopolis*. If you never cared for bugs or were frightened by "creepy crawlies," perhaps through the process of coloring you'll develop a newfound appreciation for these extrordinary animals who make our world go round.

—Peter Kuper

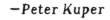

It is estimated that there are

10,000,000, 000,000, 000,000

(ten quintillion)

insects on our

planet.

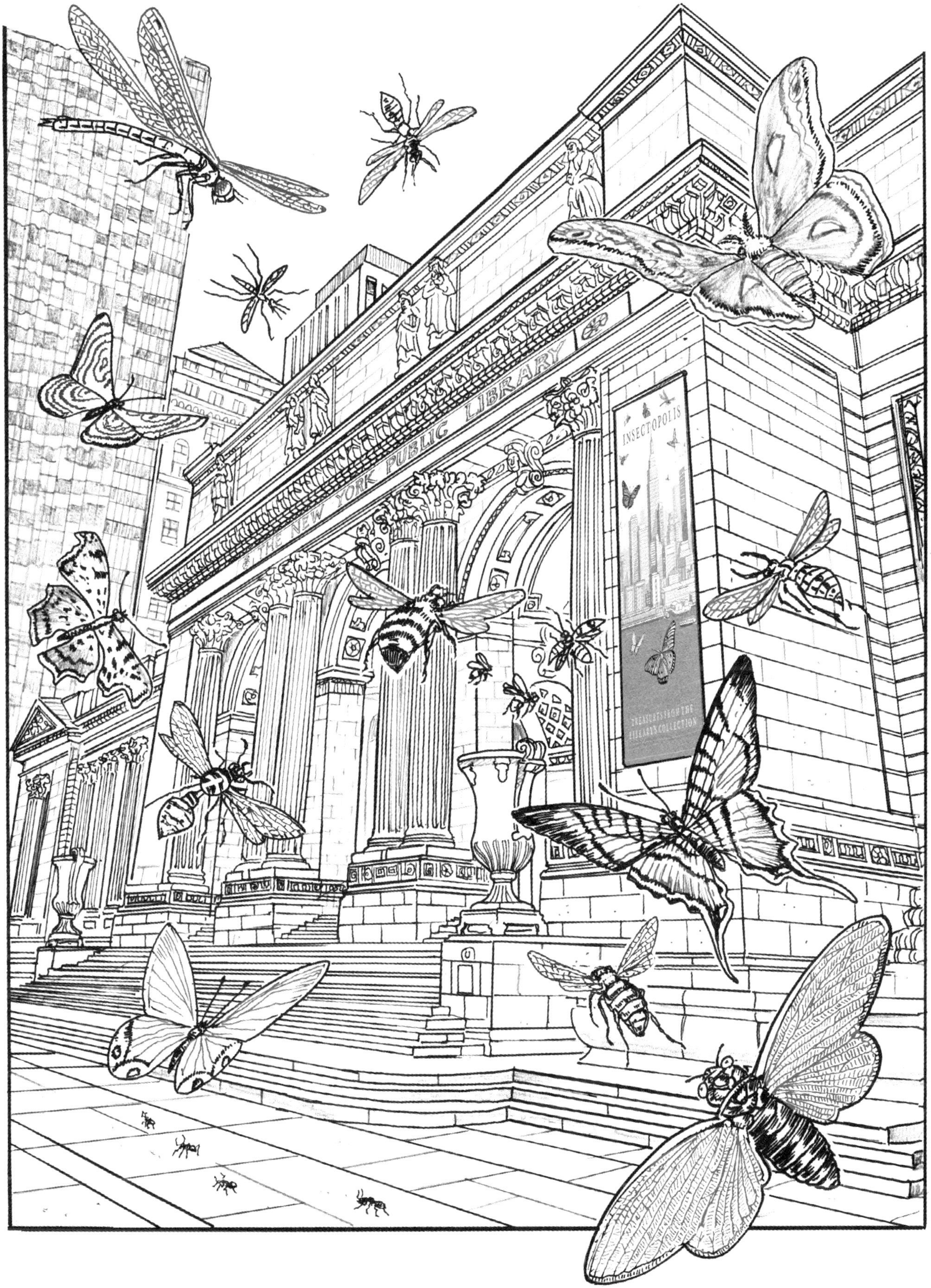
THE NEW YORK PUBLIC LIBRARY
INSECTOPOLIS

Winged insects
appeared on Earth
about 400 million
years ago (mya).

They were the first
animals to achieve
flight.

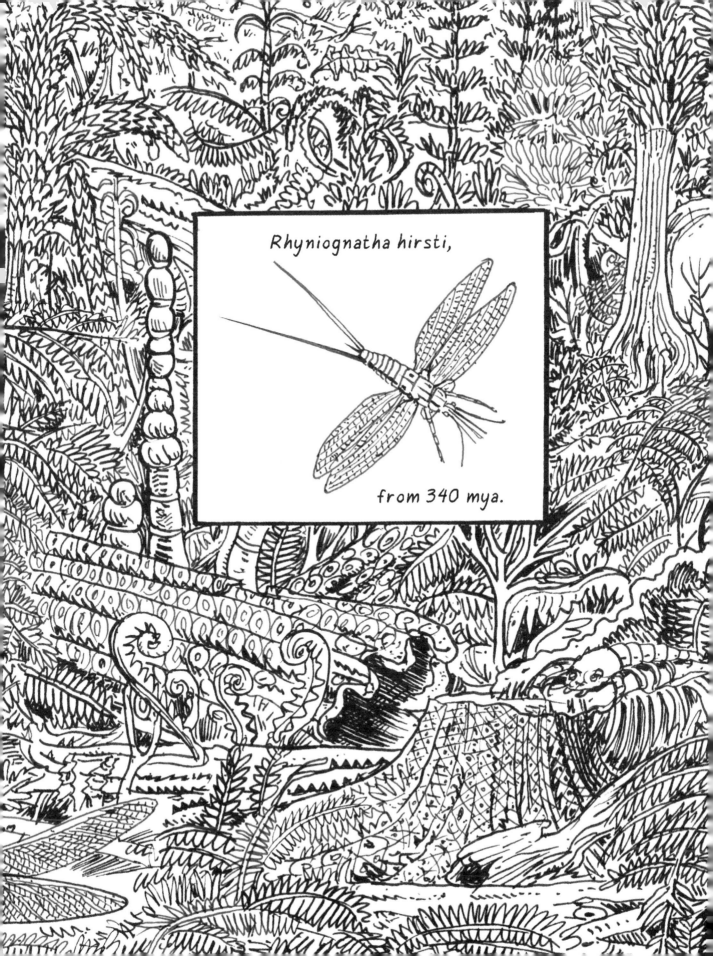

Rhyniognatha hirsti, from 340 mya.

"If all mankind were to disappear,
the world would regenerate back to the rich state
of equilibrium that existed ten thousand years ago.

If insects were to vanish,

the environment would
collapse into chaos."

—E. O. Wilson
(1929-2021)
from
Sociobiology

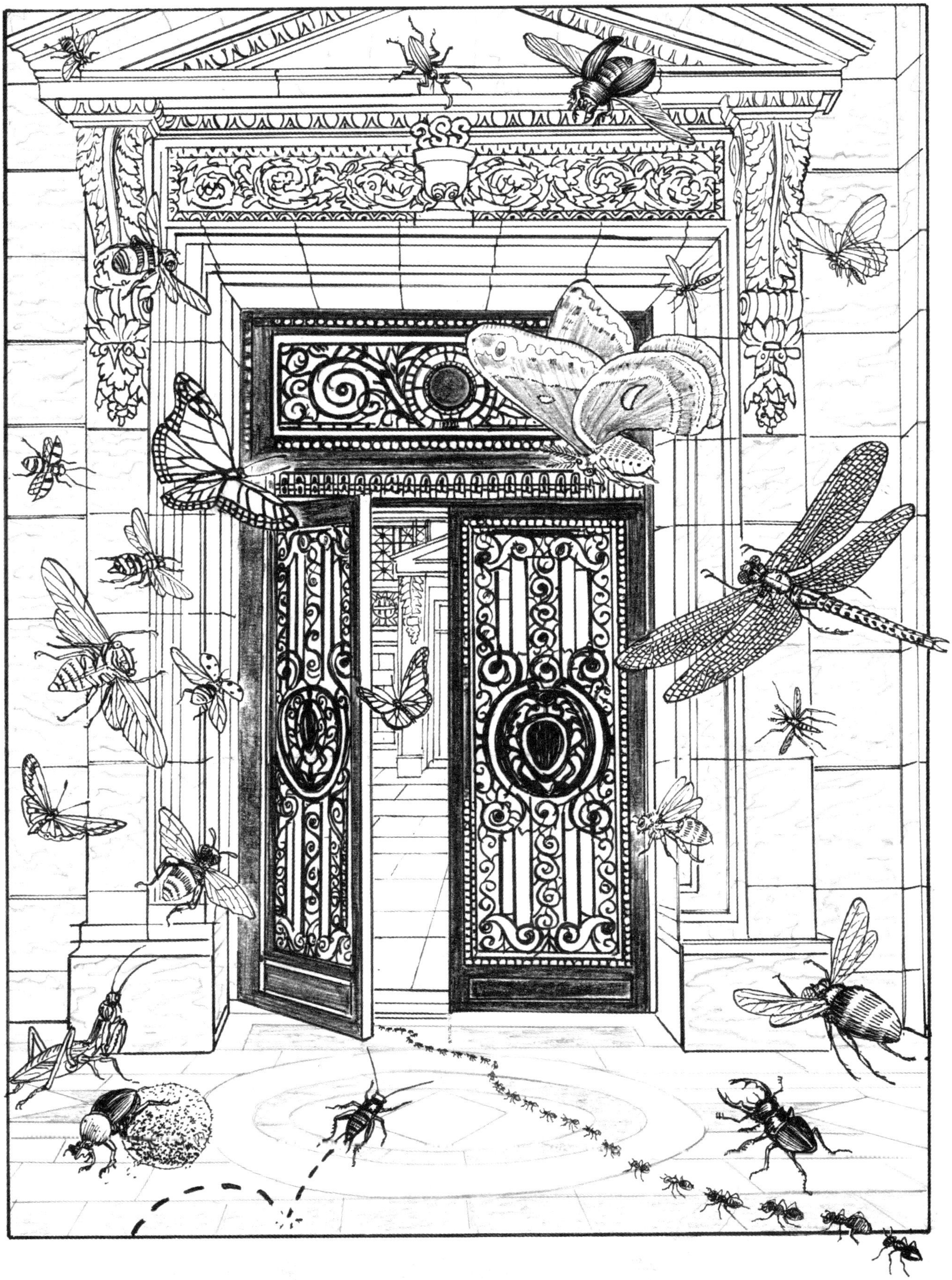

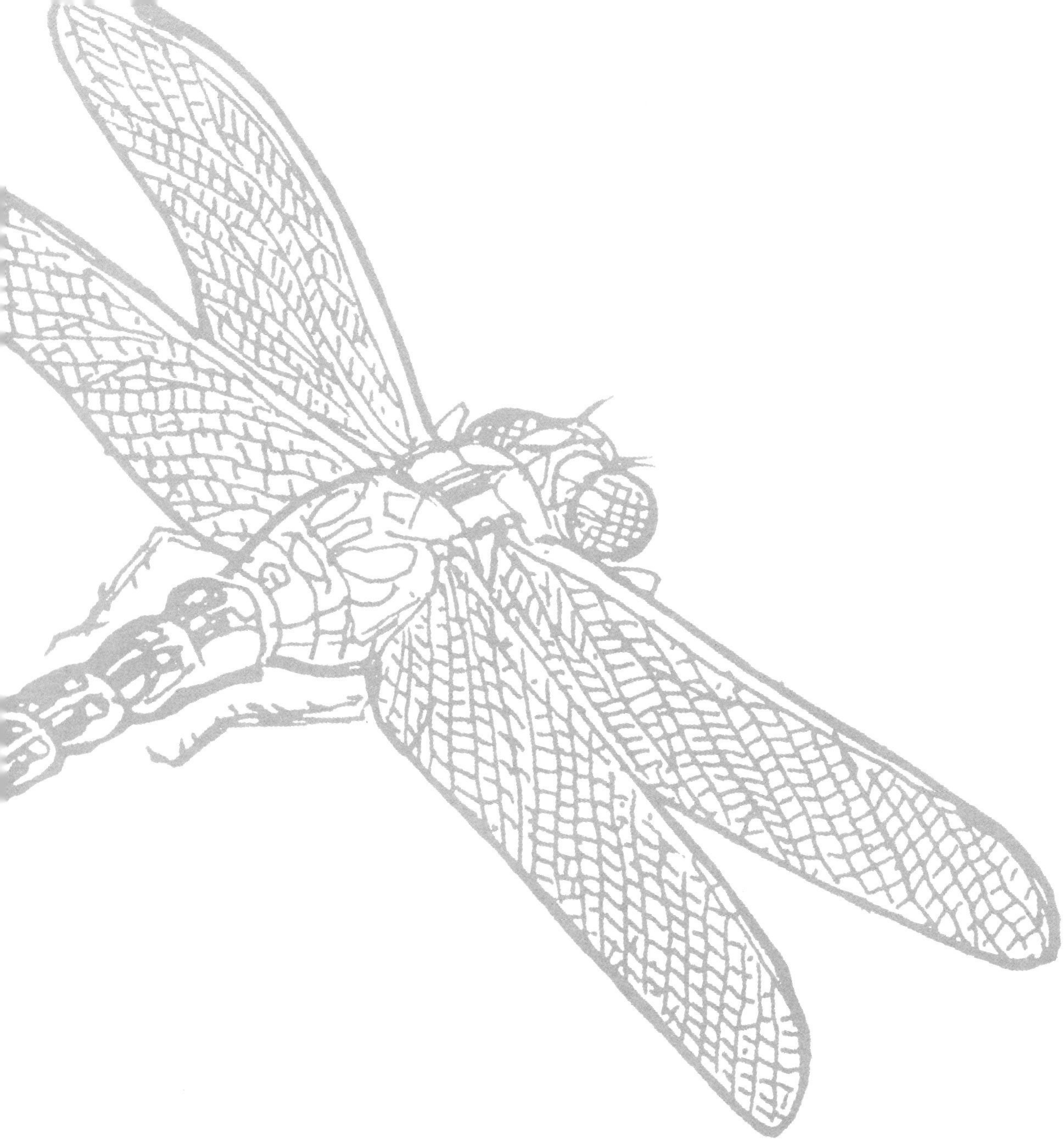

Griffinflies, also known as Meganisoptera, were giant dragonfly-like insects that lived about 300 million years ago . . .

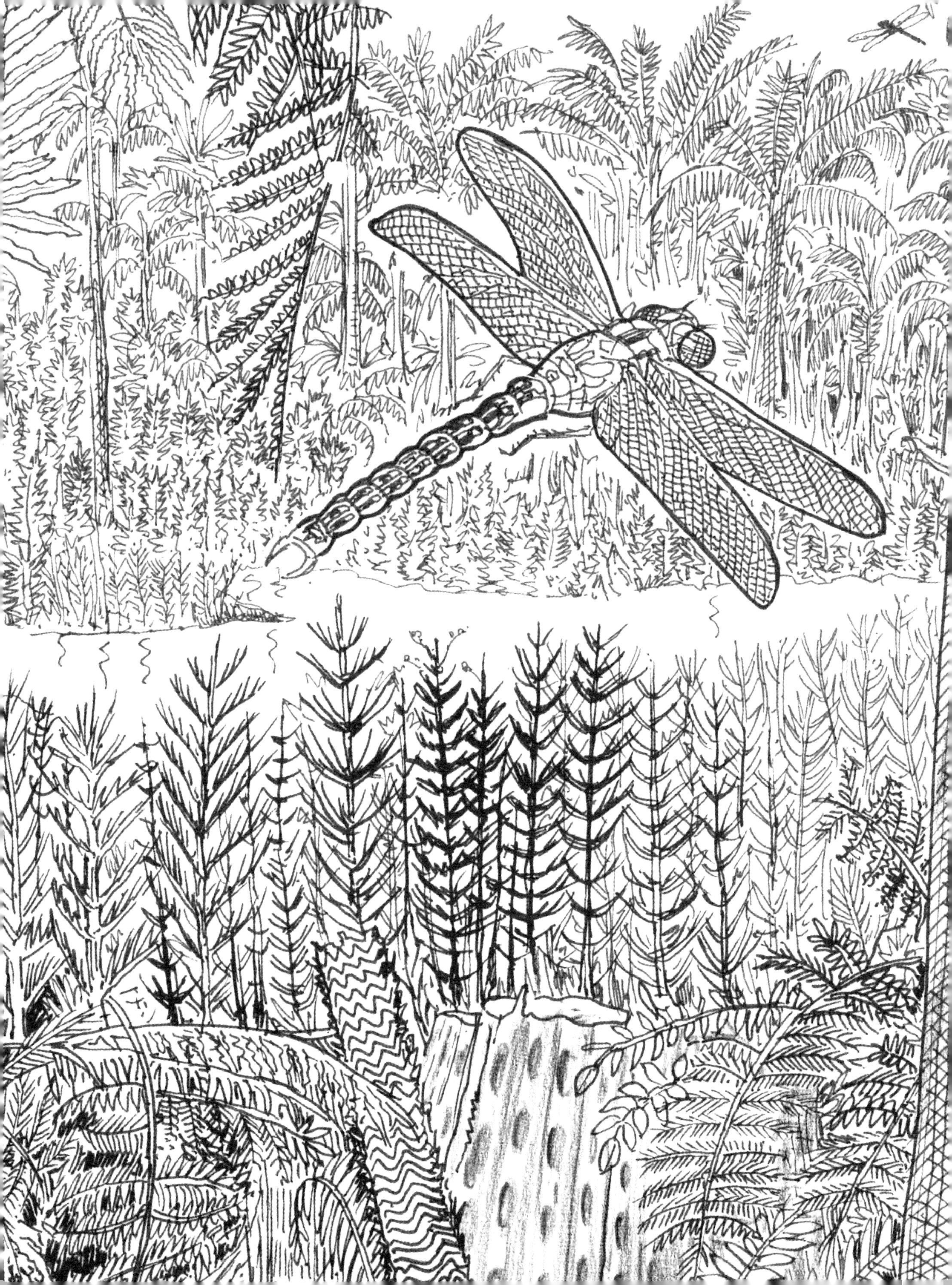

They lived during the
Carboniferous Period and had a
wingspan of up to twenty-eight inches.

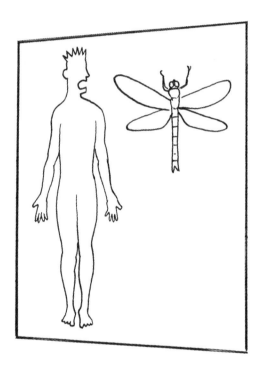

That's the size of a hawk.

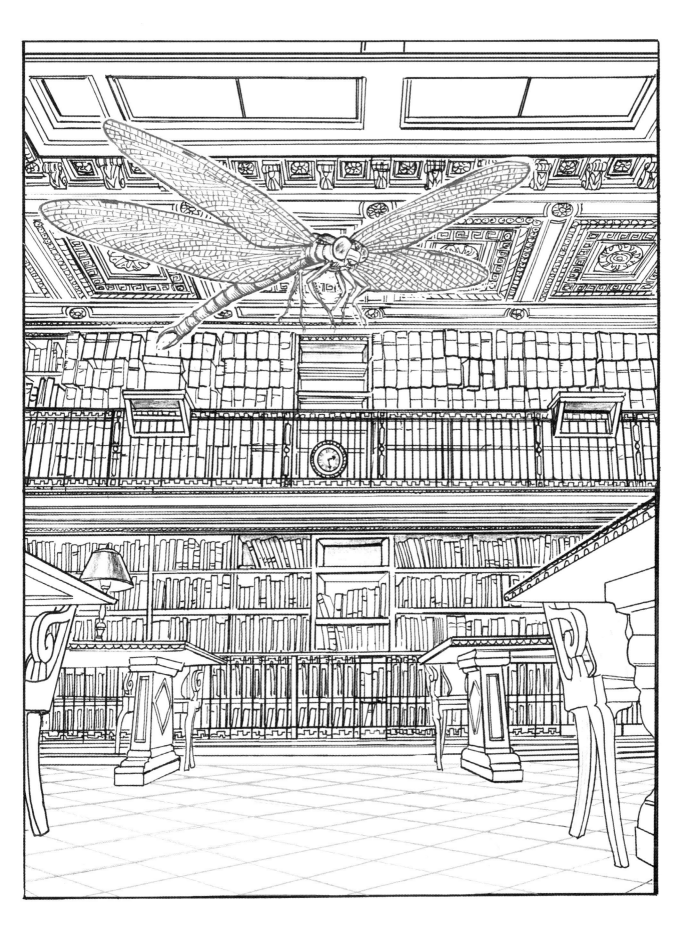

Three-fourths of the world's flowering plants and about 35 percent of the world's food crops depend on insect pollinators. After bees, the second biggest pollinators are...

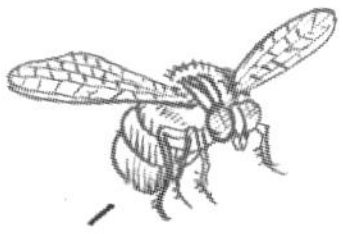

... flies.

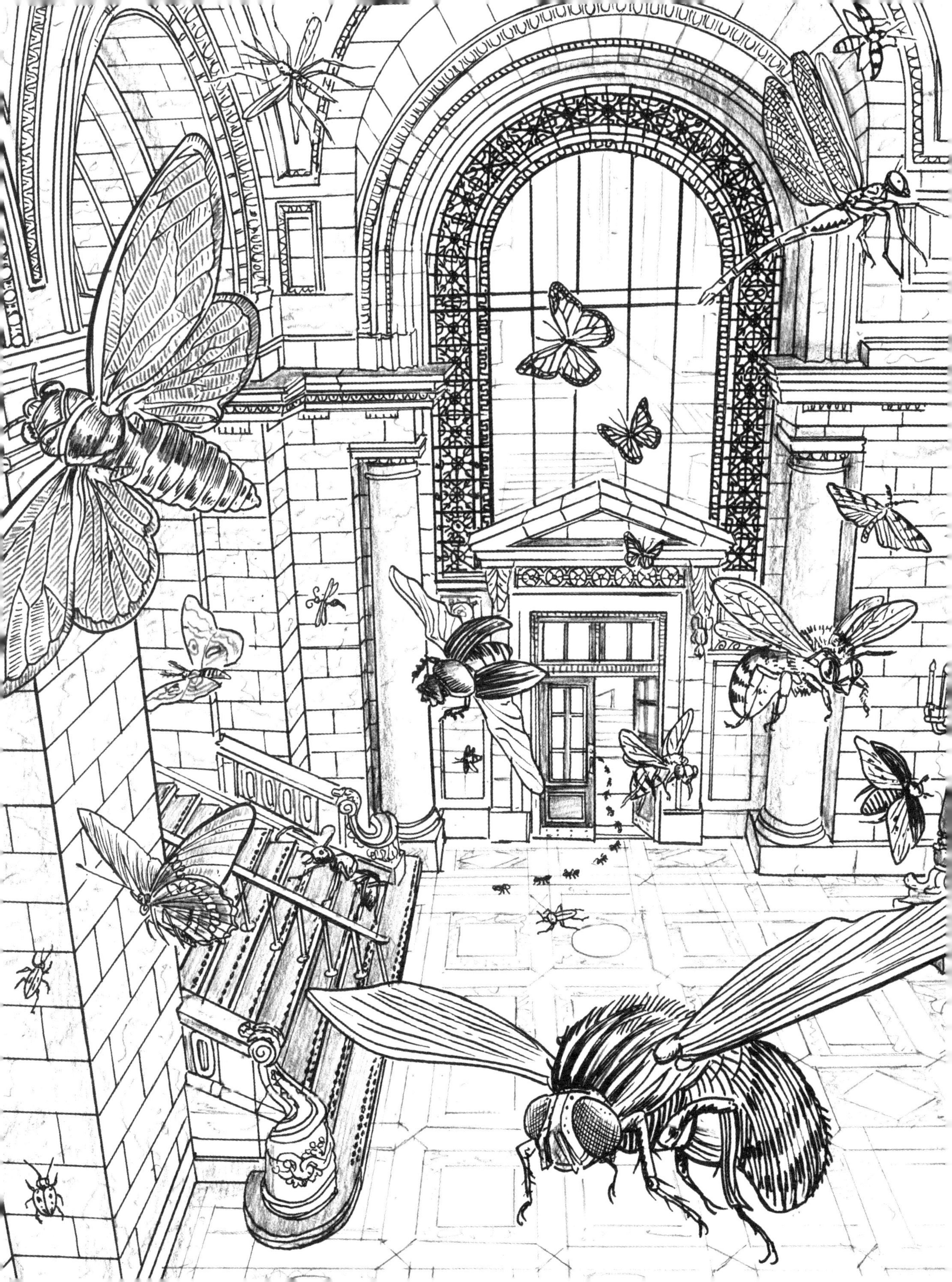

A monarch butterfly
can travel over
fifty miles
a day.

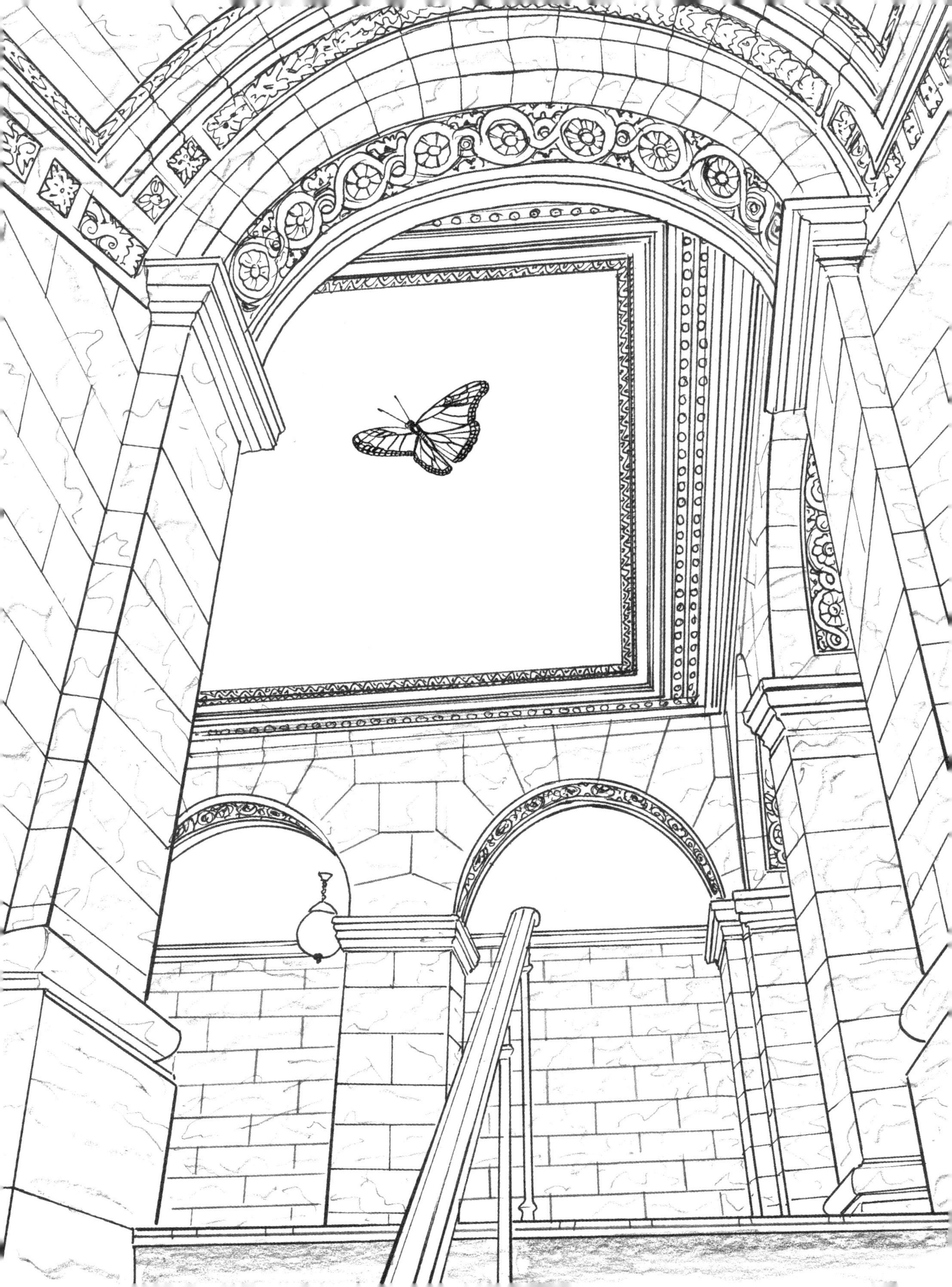

Scientists have determined
that there are at least
20 quadrillion ants
on Earth.

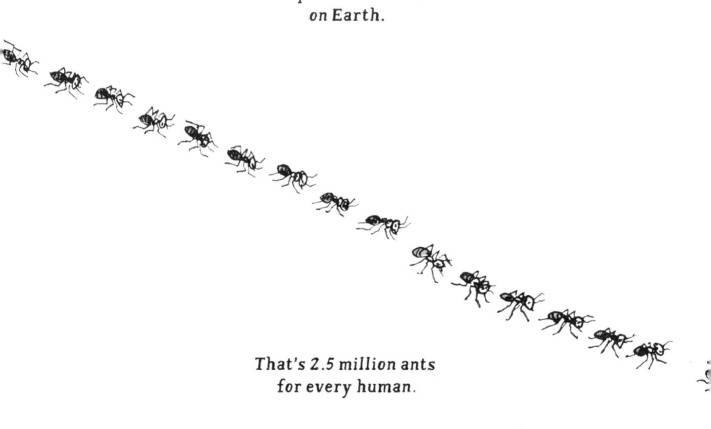

That's 2.5 million ants
for every human.

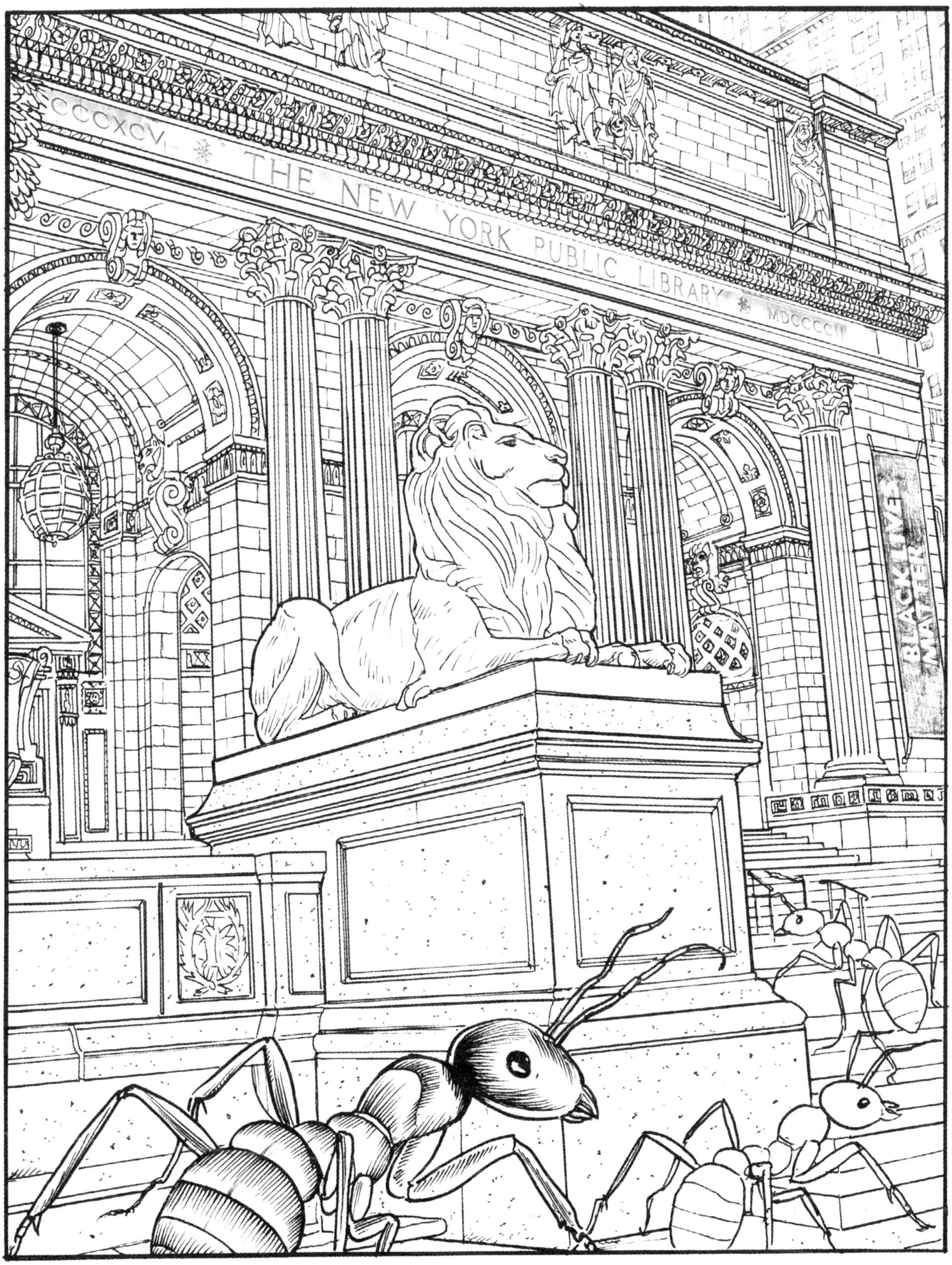
CCCXCV
THE NEW YORK PUBLIC LIBRARY
MDCCCCII

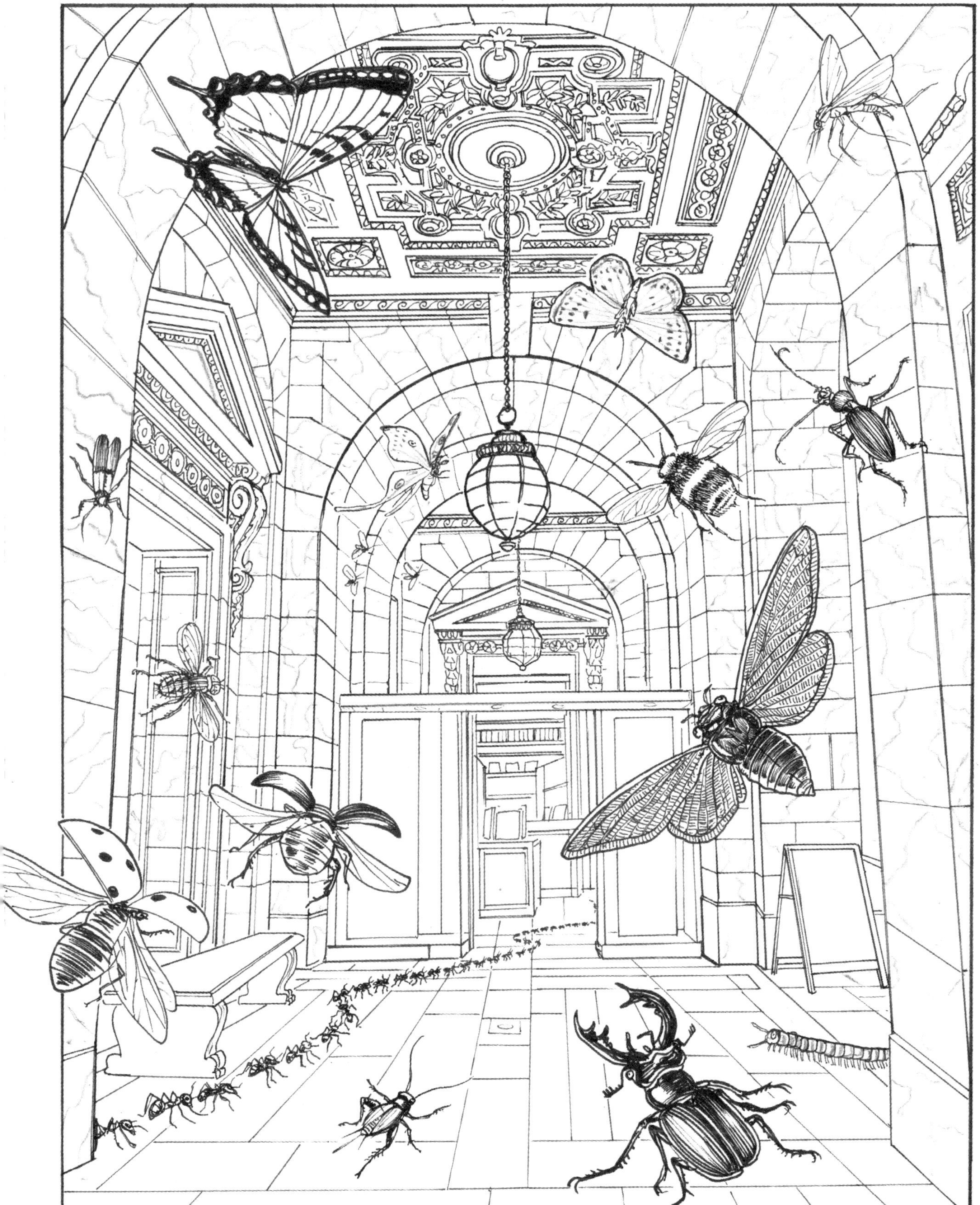

During the Creteceous Period,
insect pollinators played a crucial
role in the proliferation
of flowering plants
across the globe.

Over time, flowers developed
brighter colors, enticing scents,
and other traits to attract pollinators;
insects coevolved to take advantage
of this new food source.

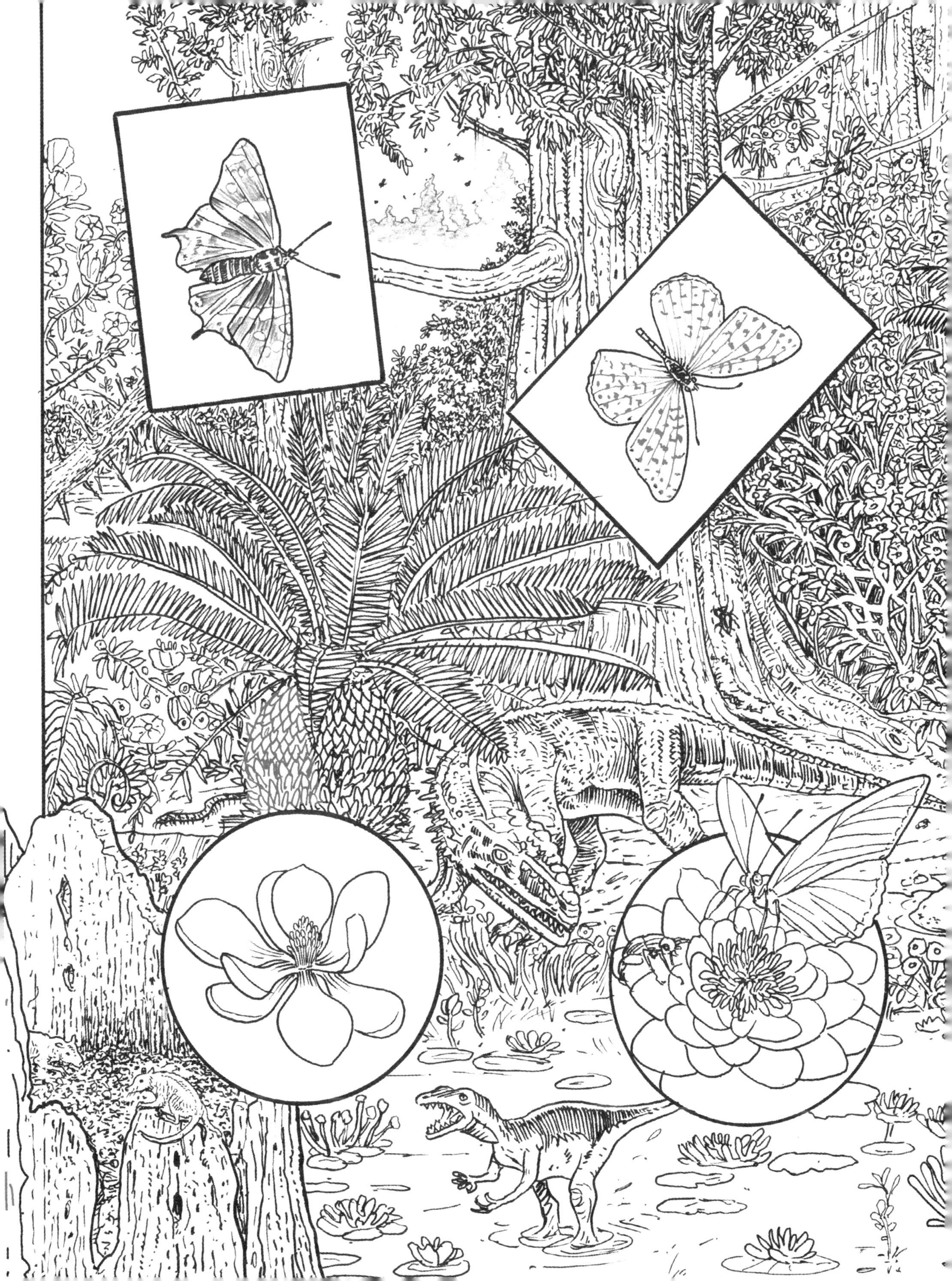

"And wisdom
is a butterfly
and not a gloomy
bird of prey."

—W. B. Yeats
(1865–1939)
from his poem
Tom O'Roughley

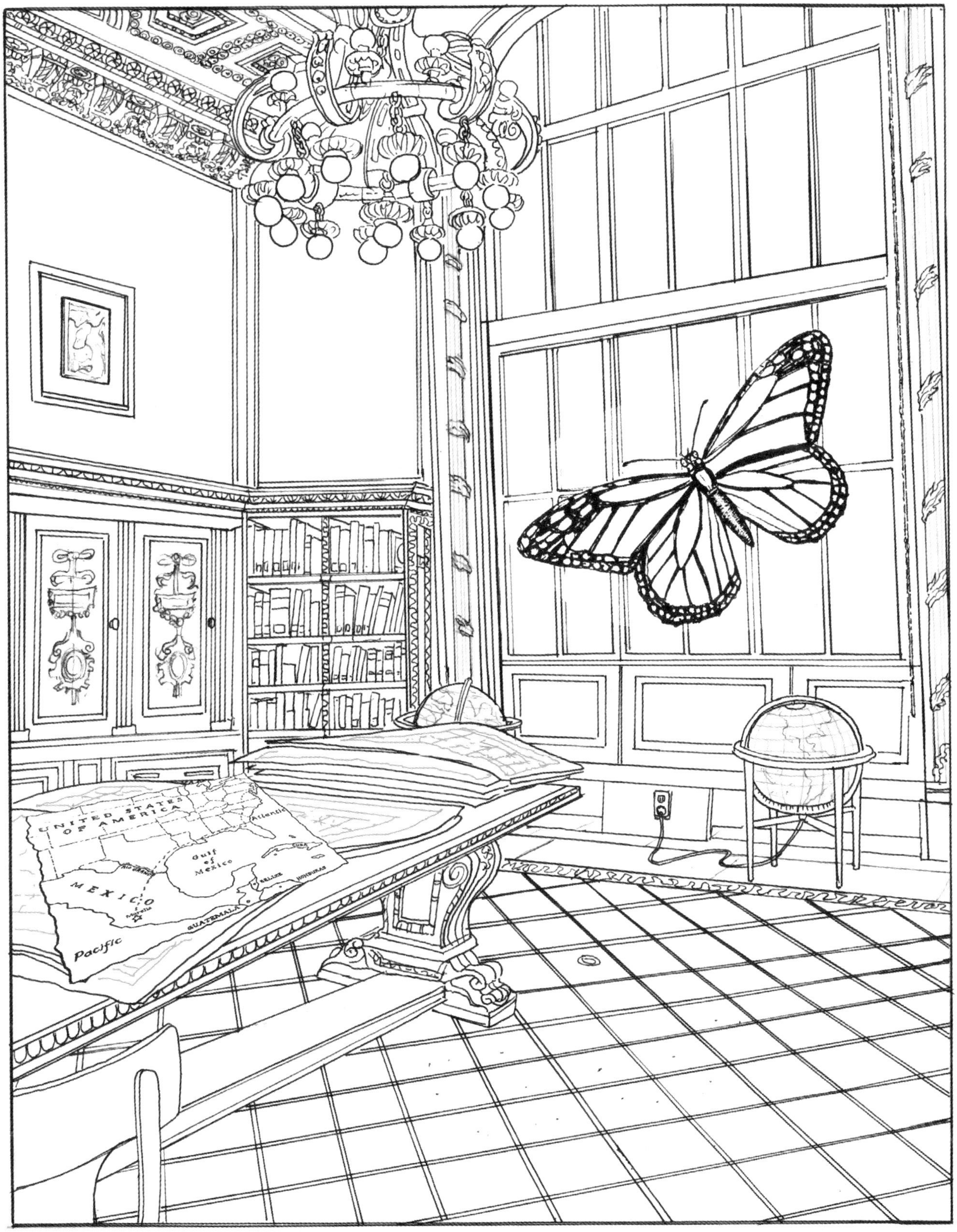
UNITED STATES OF AMERICA
Atlantic
Gulf of Mexico
RIO GRANDE
MEXICO
Morelia
BELIZE
HONDURAS
GUATEMALA
Pacific

Every fall,

monarchs
migrate

from
North America...

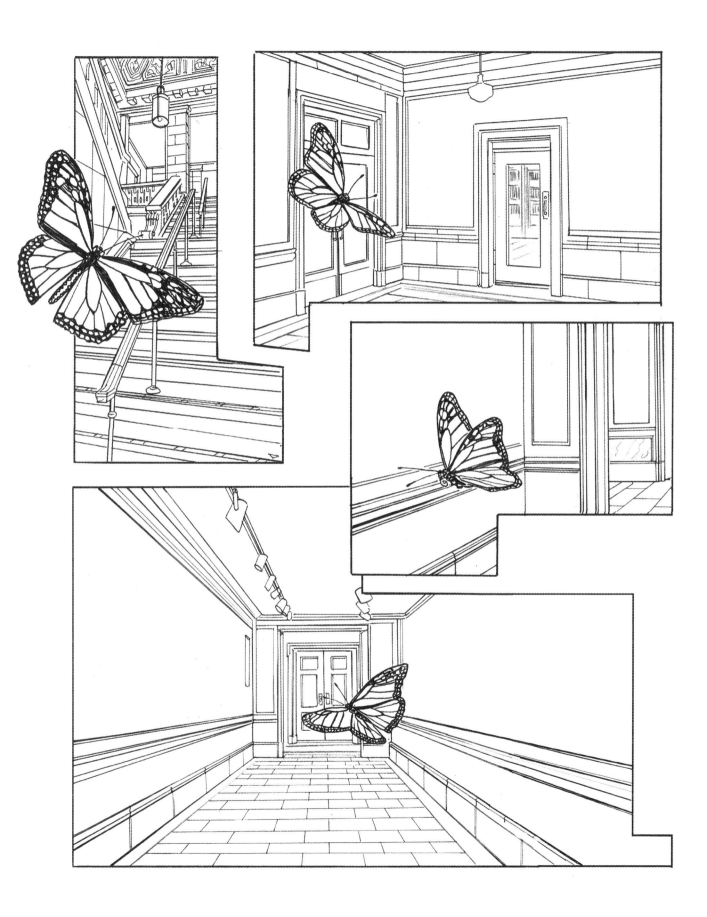

... to one particular area of pine forests in Mexico...

a nearly three-thousand-mile journey.

They use their antennae as a compass to sense the Earth's magnetic field.

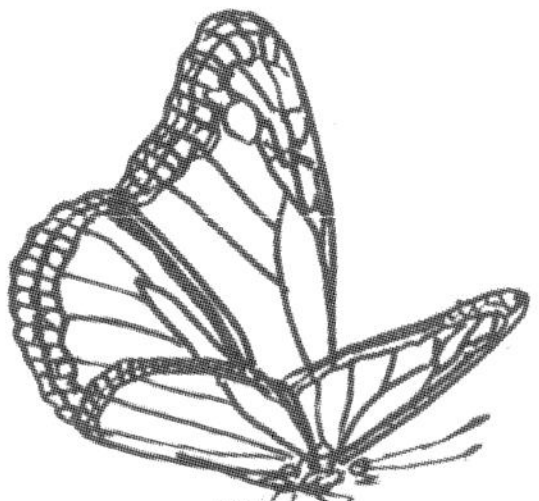

Though, precisely what guides them to their destination remains a mystery.

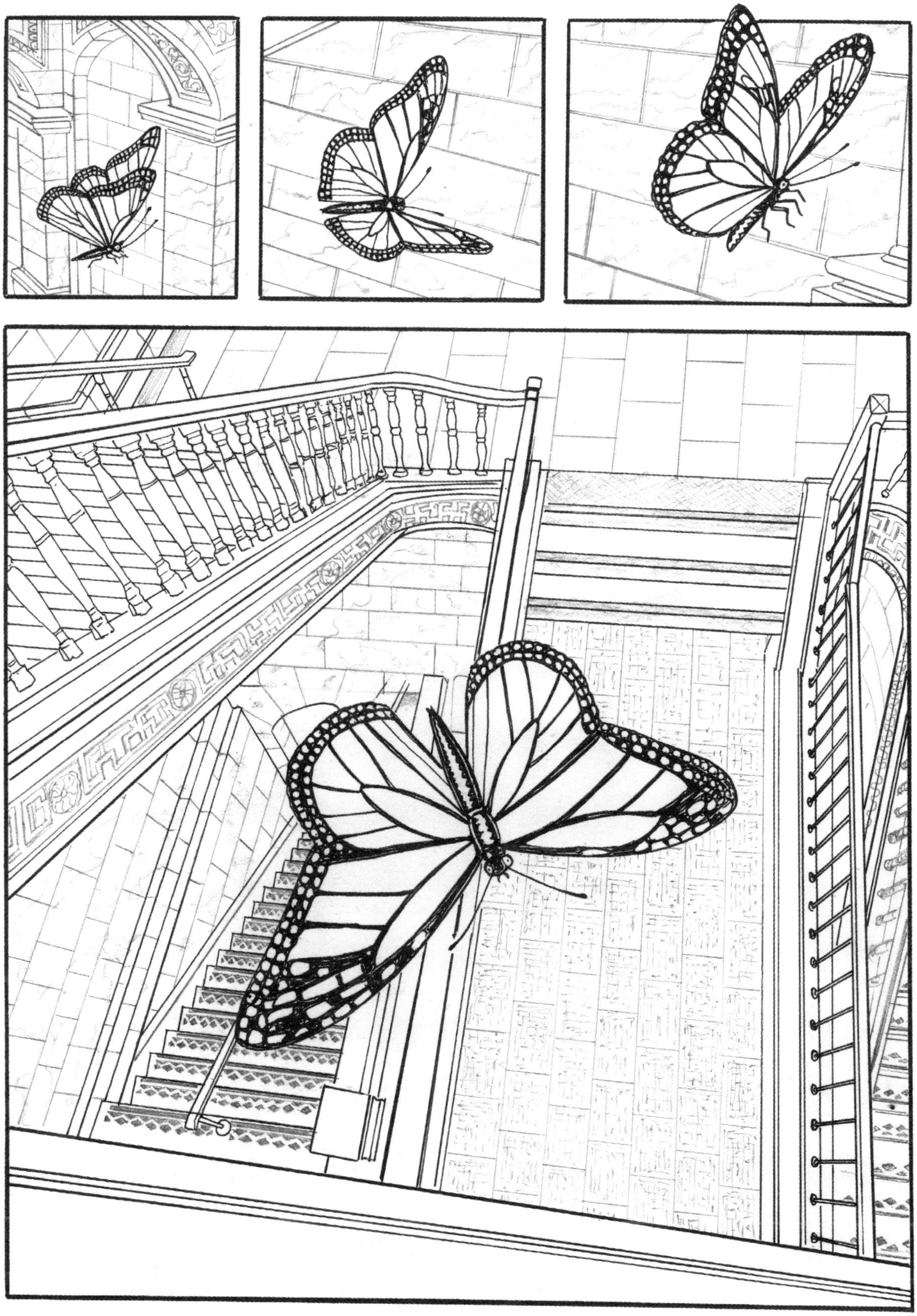

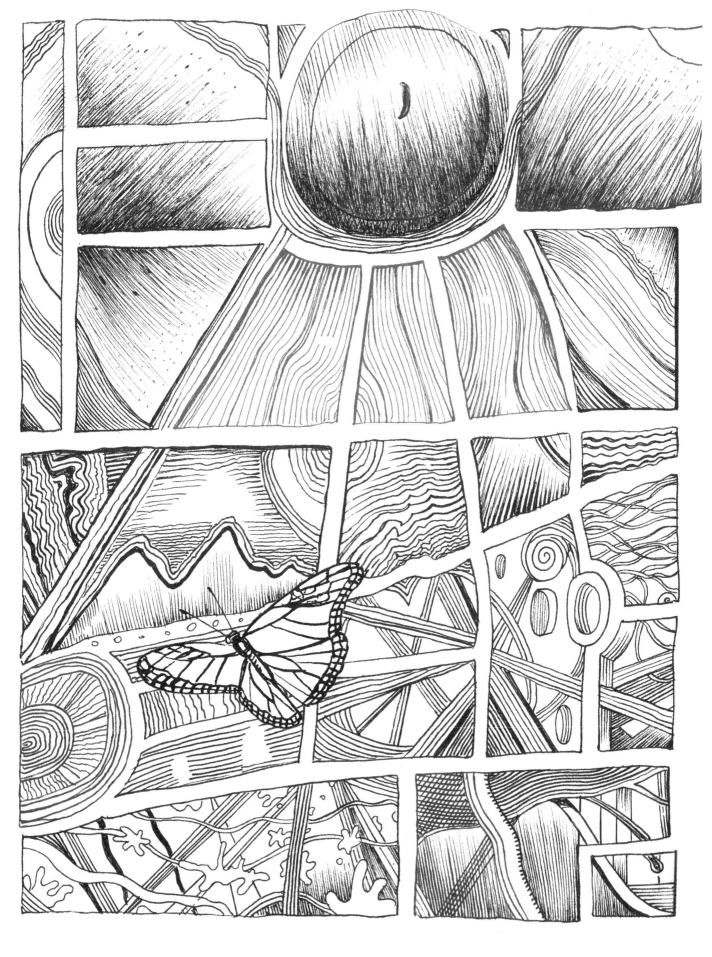

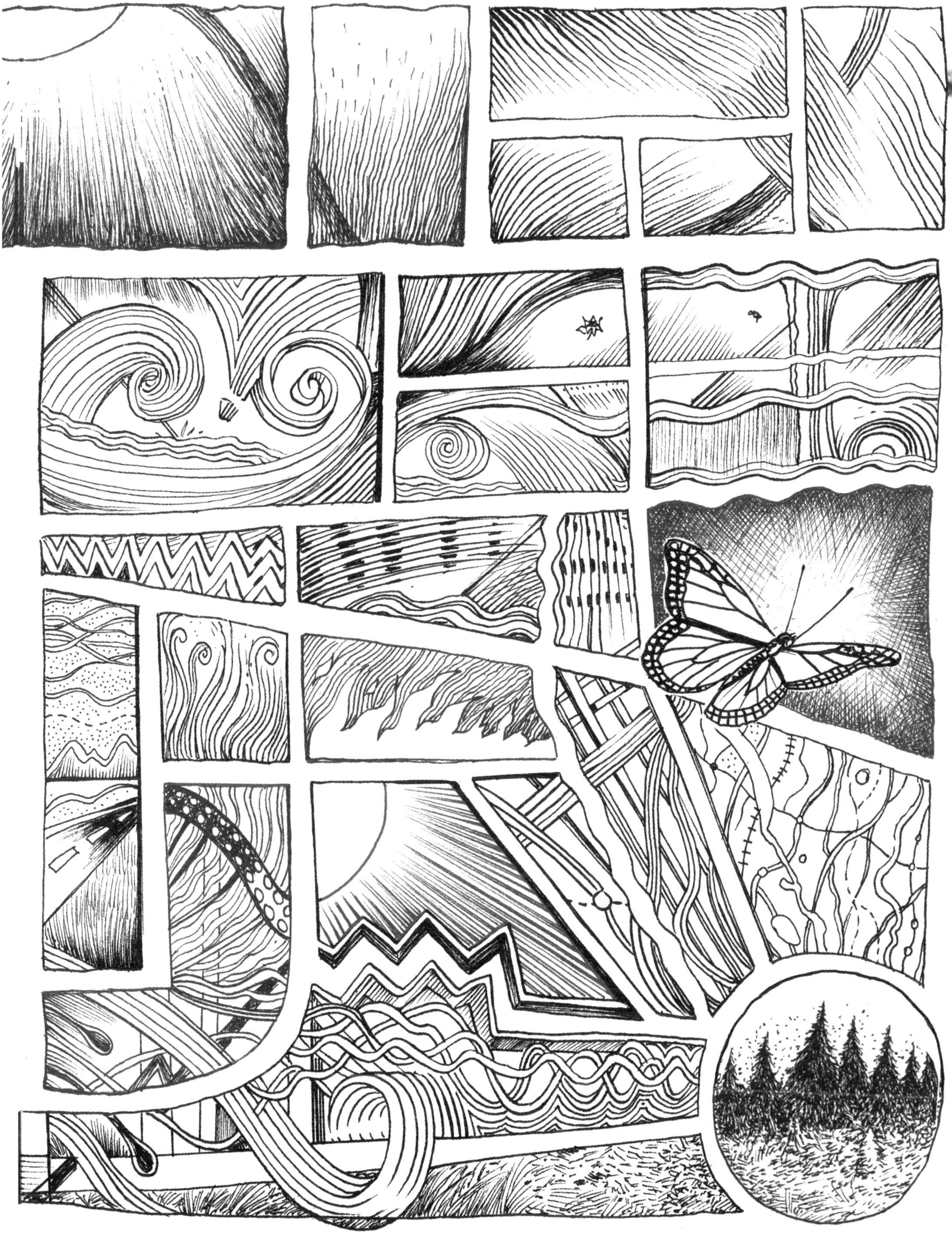

Bees
and
ants
evolved
from

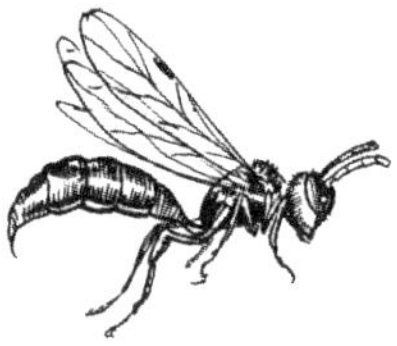

wasps.

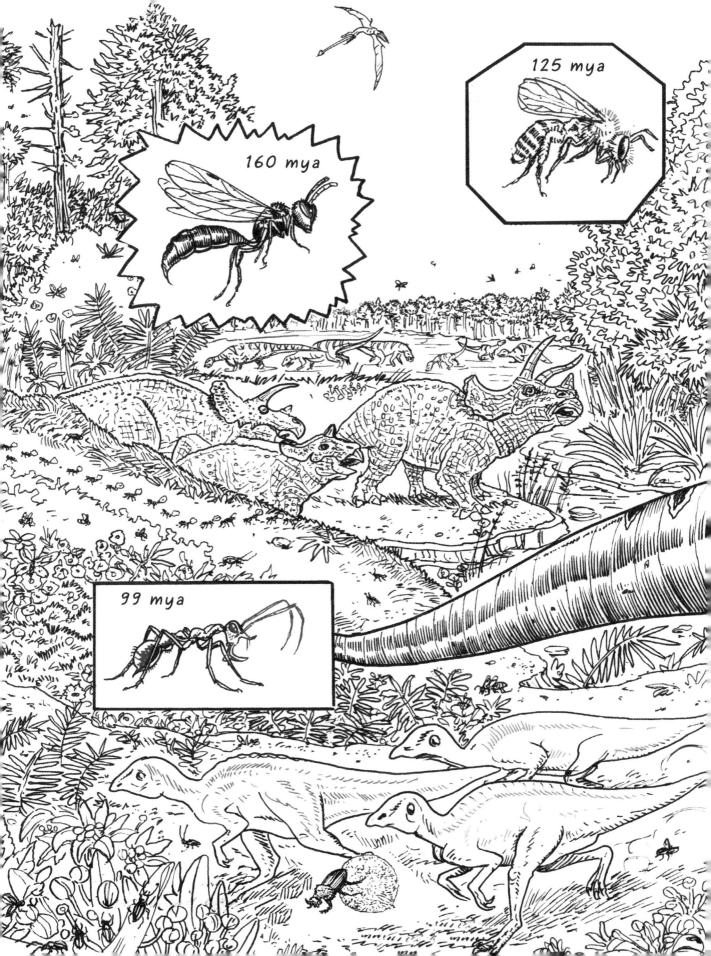

160 mya

125 mya

99 mya

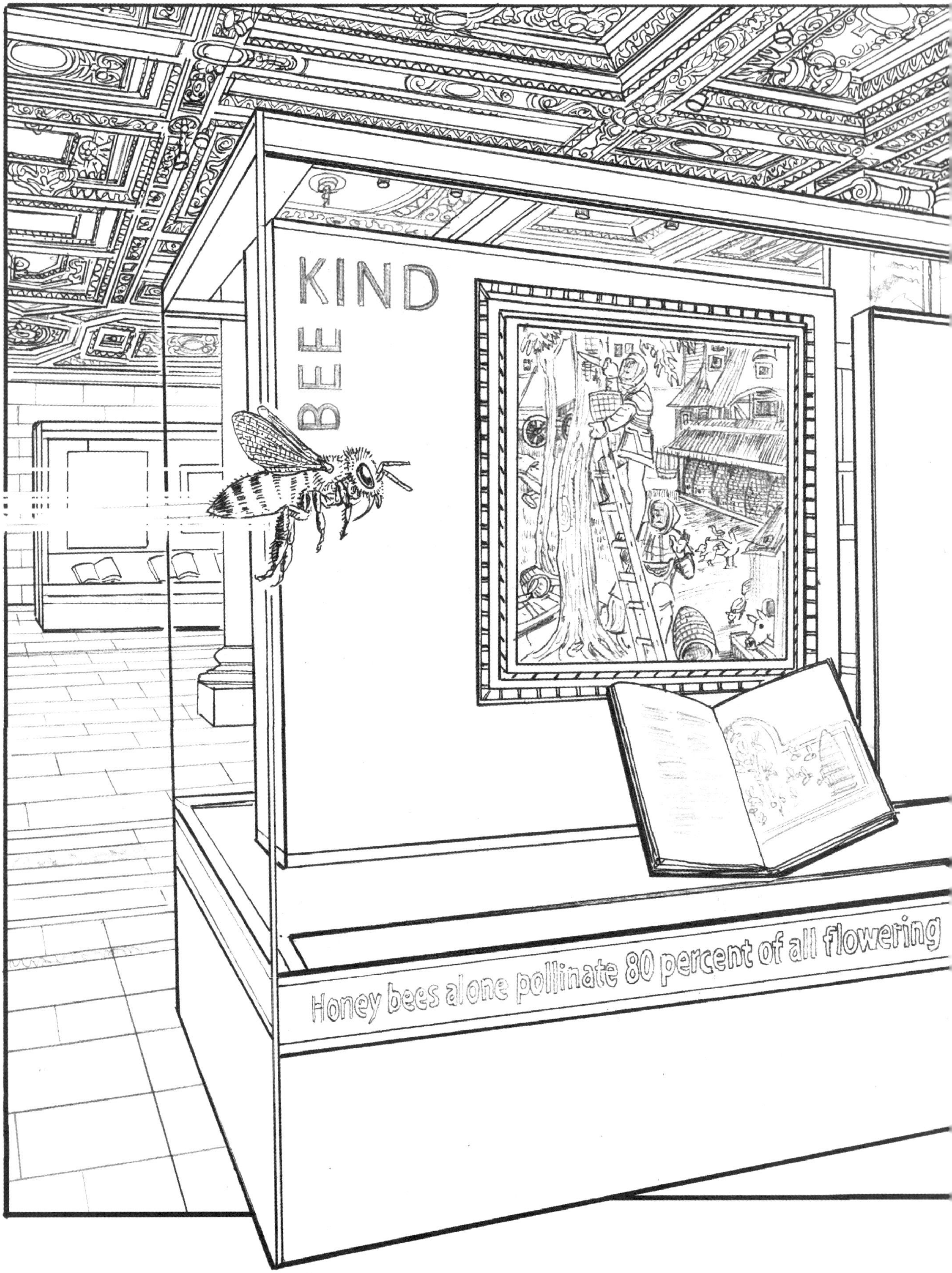

BEE KIND
Honey bees alone pollinate 80 percent of all flowering

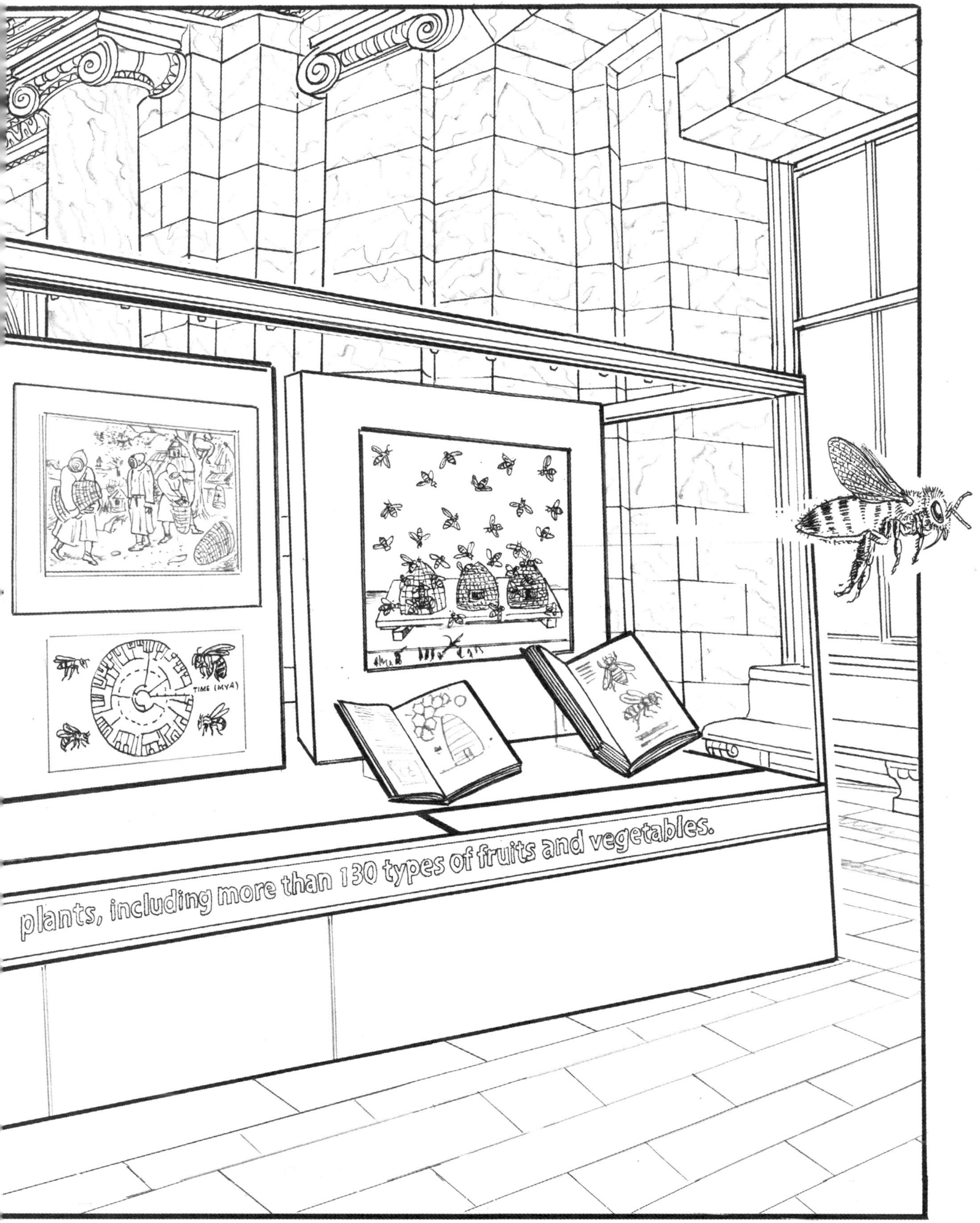

TIME (MYA)
plants, including more than 130 types of fruits and vegetables.

Beetles (*Coleoptera*)
are by far the largest order of insects.
They make up a quarter of all animal species.
There are roughly 400 thousand species of beetles,
totaling 500 quintillion individual insects.

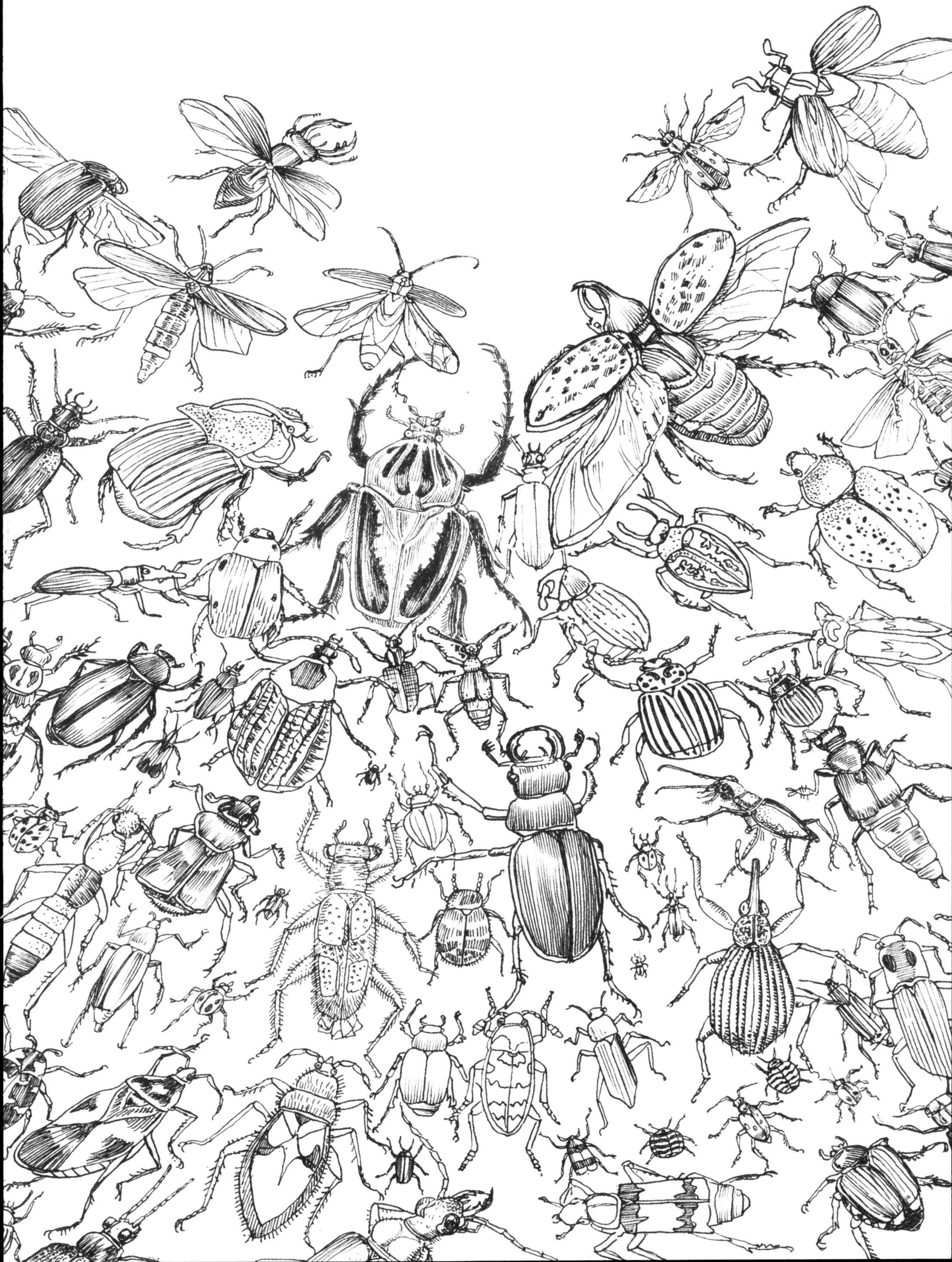

In author Franz Kafka's
1915 story, *The Metamorphosis,*
his character Gregor Samsa
awakes one morning to find
himself transformed.

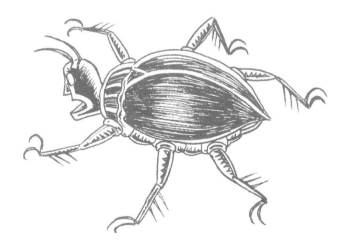

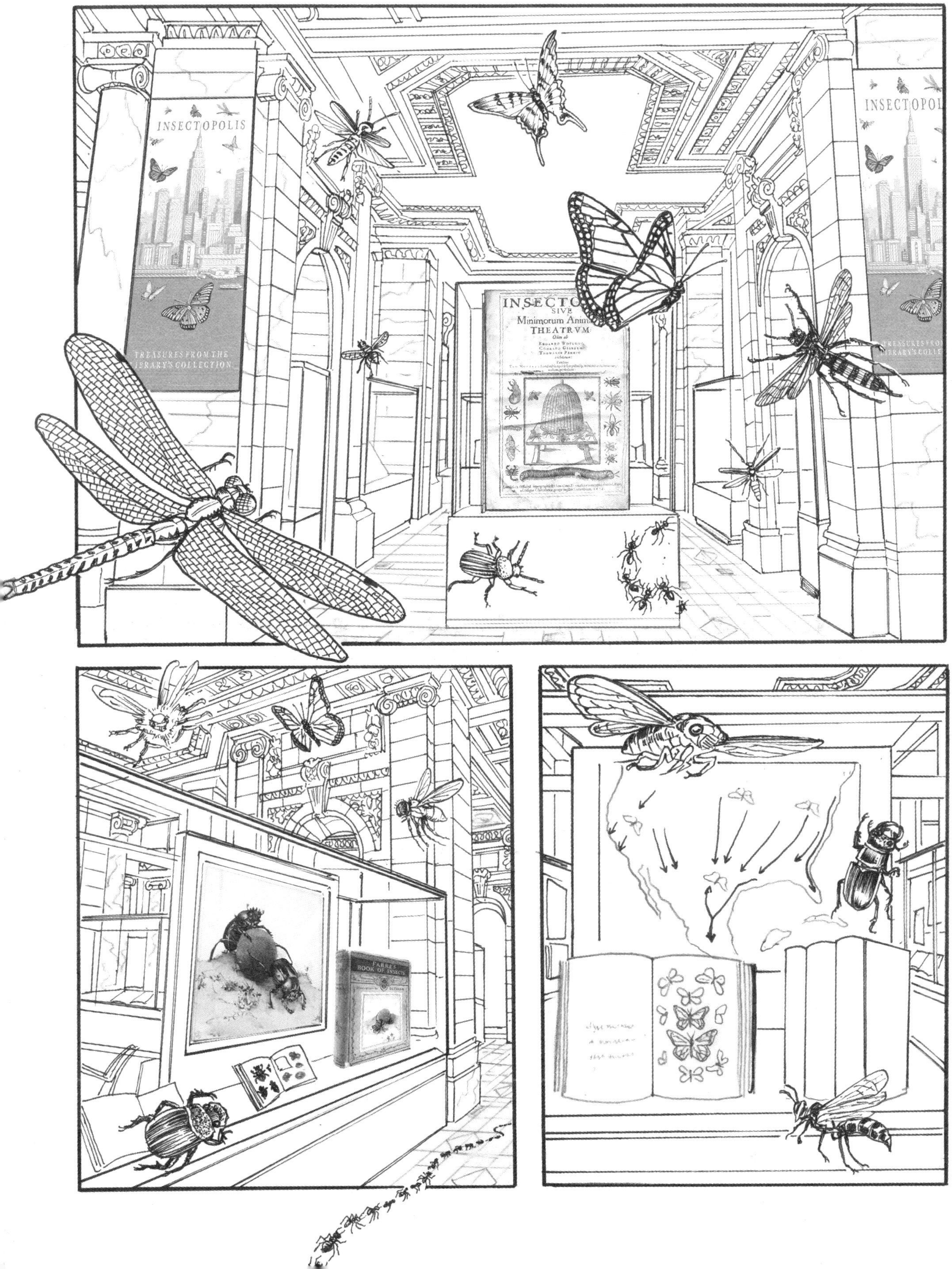
INSECTOPOLIS
TREASURES FROM THE LIBRARY'S COLLECTION
INSECTOPOLIS
TREASURES FROM THE LIBRARY'S COLLECTION
INSECTO
SIVE
Minimorum Anim
THEATRVM
FABRE'S BOOK OF INSECTS

MOTHERS OF ENTOMOLOGY

Maria Sibylla Merian

Eleanor Ormerod
(1828-1901)
American
Mother of
Agricultural
Entomology

Maria Sibylla Merian
(1647-1717)
German
Mother of
Entomology,
Naturalist,and
Illustrator

Anna Comstock
(1864-1930)
American
Pioneering
Insect Illustrator
and Author

Mary Talbot
(1903-1990)
American
Mother of
Myrmecology
(the study of ants)

Miriam Rothschild
(1908-2005)
British
World Authority
on Fleas, Butterfiles,
Pyrazines, and
Chemical Communication

Maria Sibylla Merian

THE NATURAL HISTORY OF THE ANTS
OF MICHIGAN'S E. S. GEORGE RESERVE:
A 26 YEAR STUDY

Handbook of
NATURE STUDY
By Anna Botsford Comstock

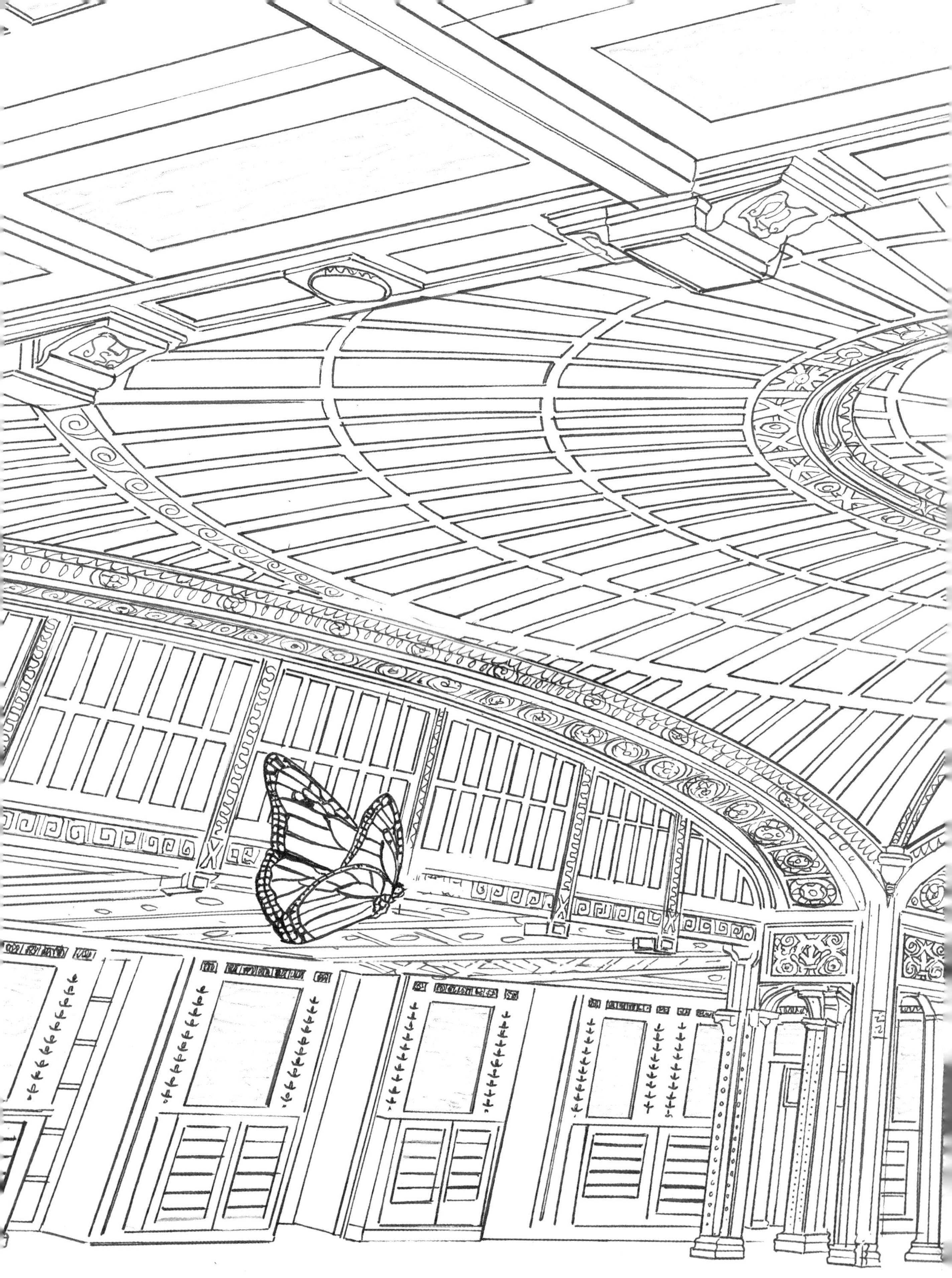

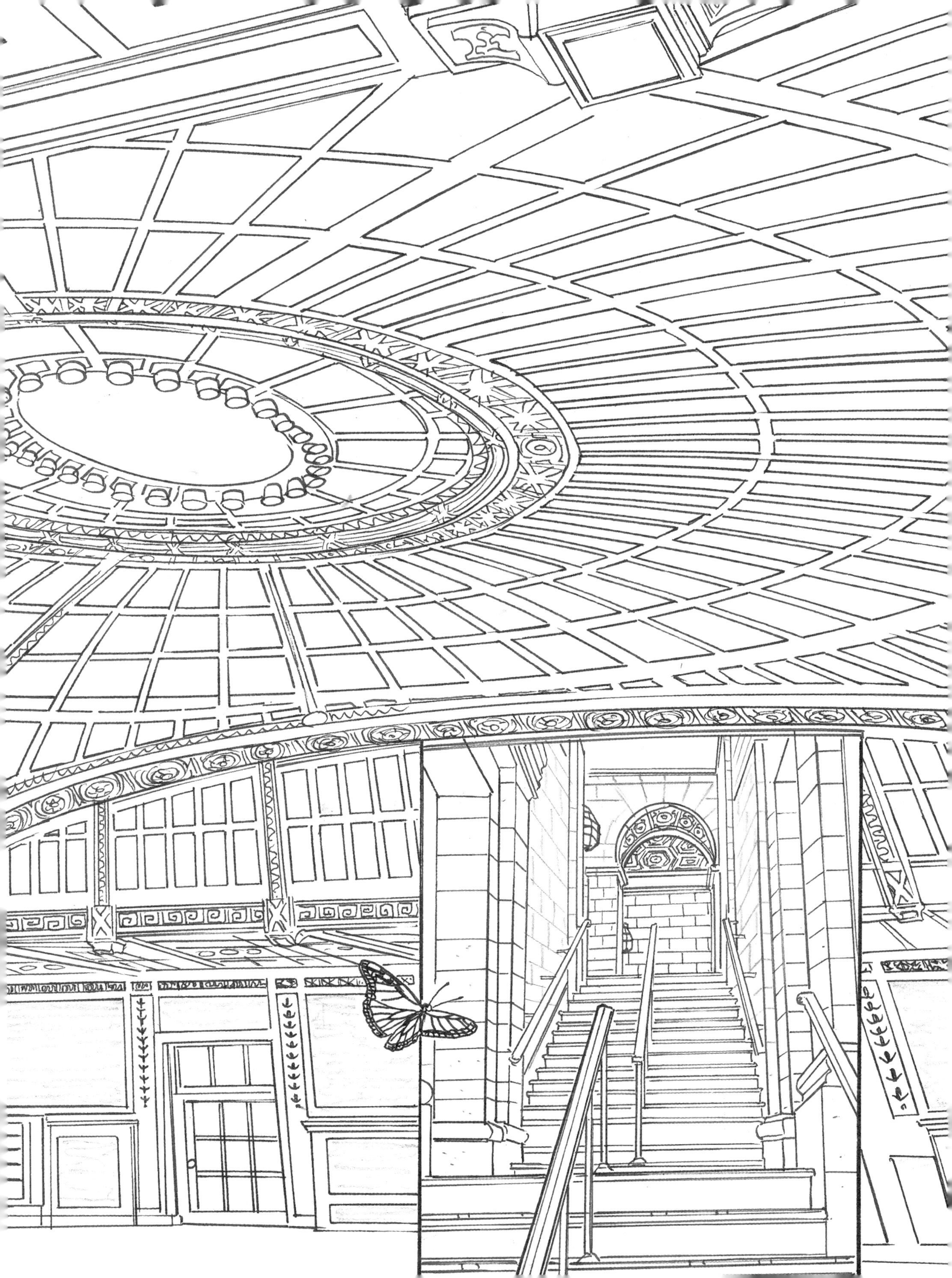

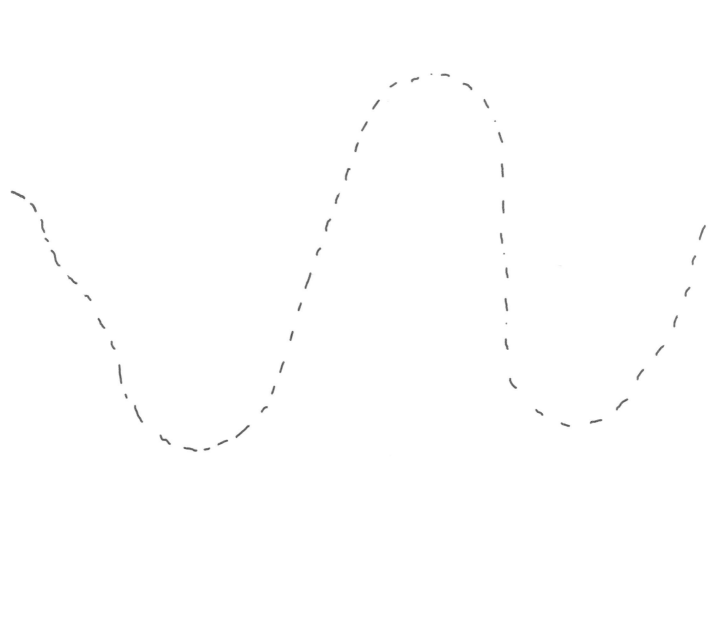

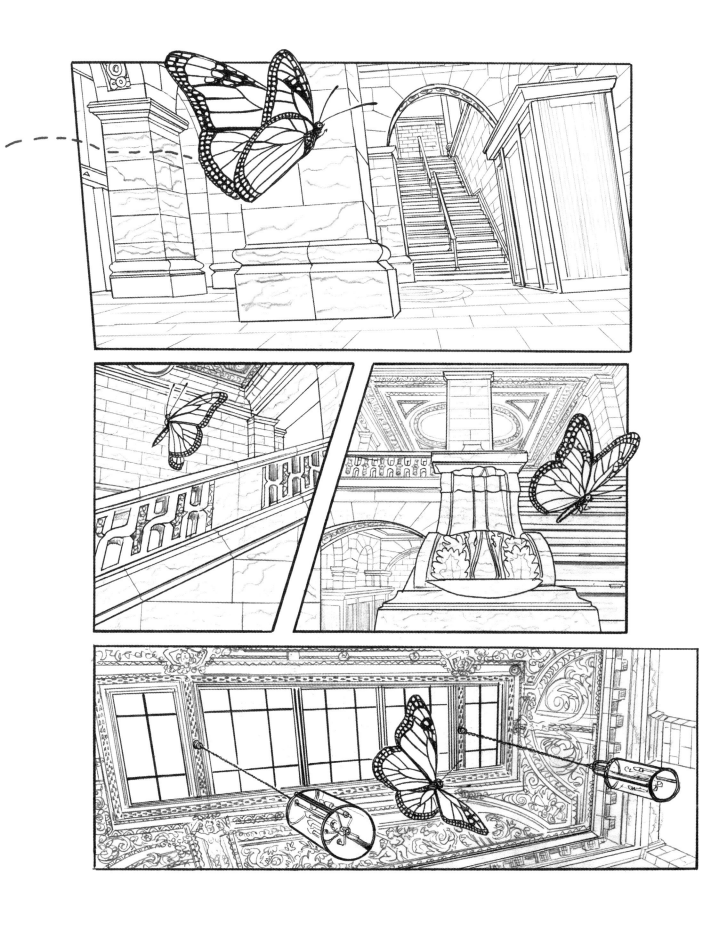

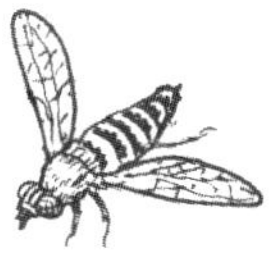

The Eocene is a
geological epoch that
lasted from about
56 to 33.9 million years ago.

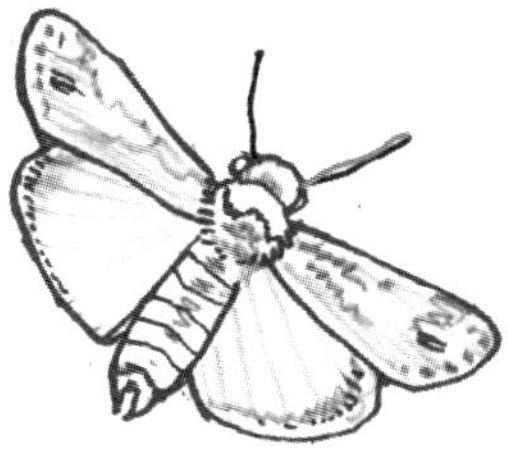

At the beginning of the Eocene,
Earth's temperature rose sharply,
causing mass extinctions.

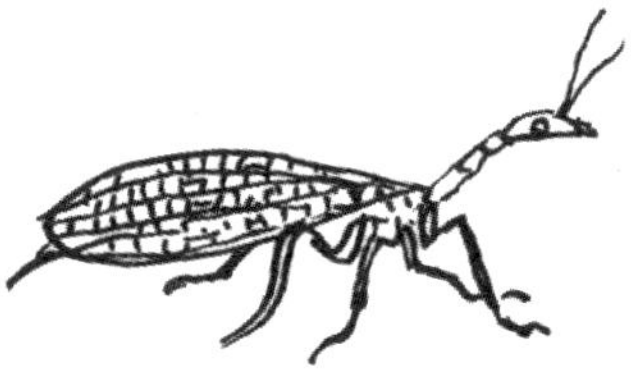

In the middle period, as the world
cooled, new species evolved
and insects thrived.

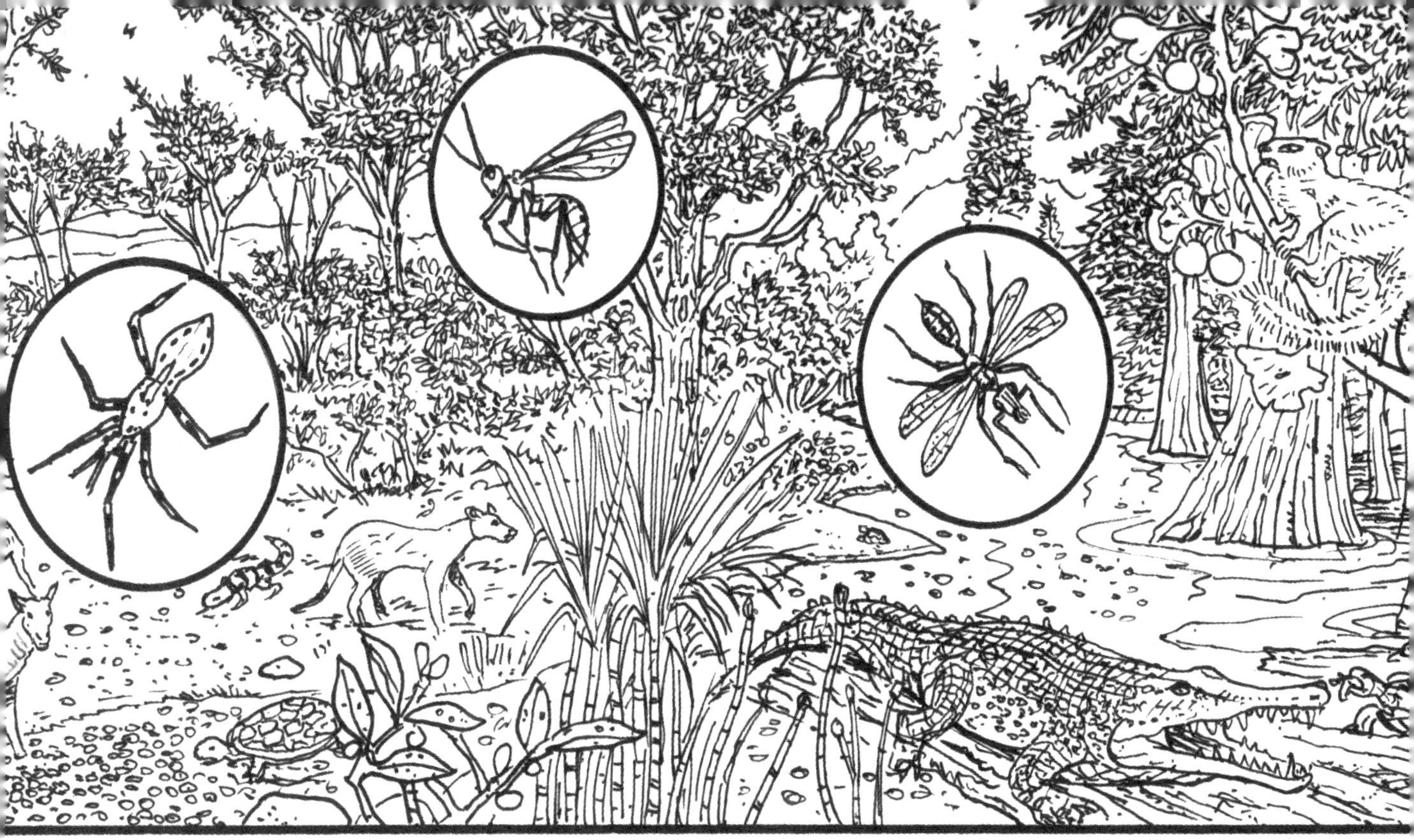

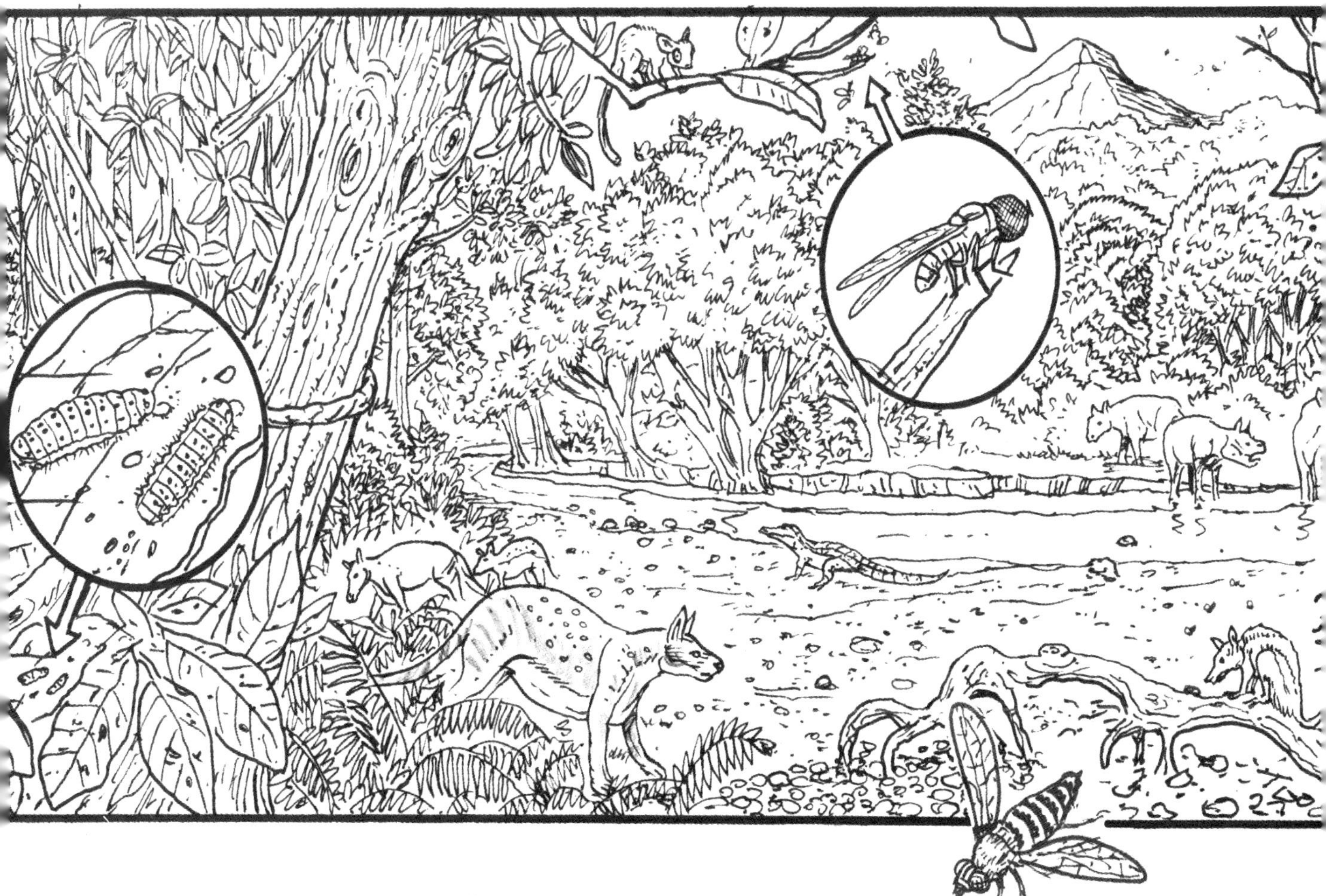

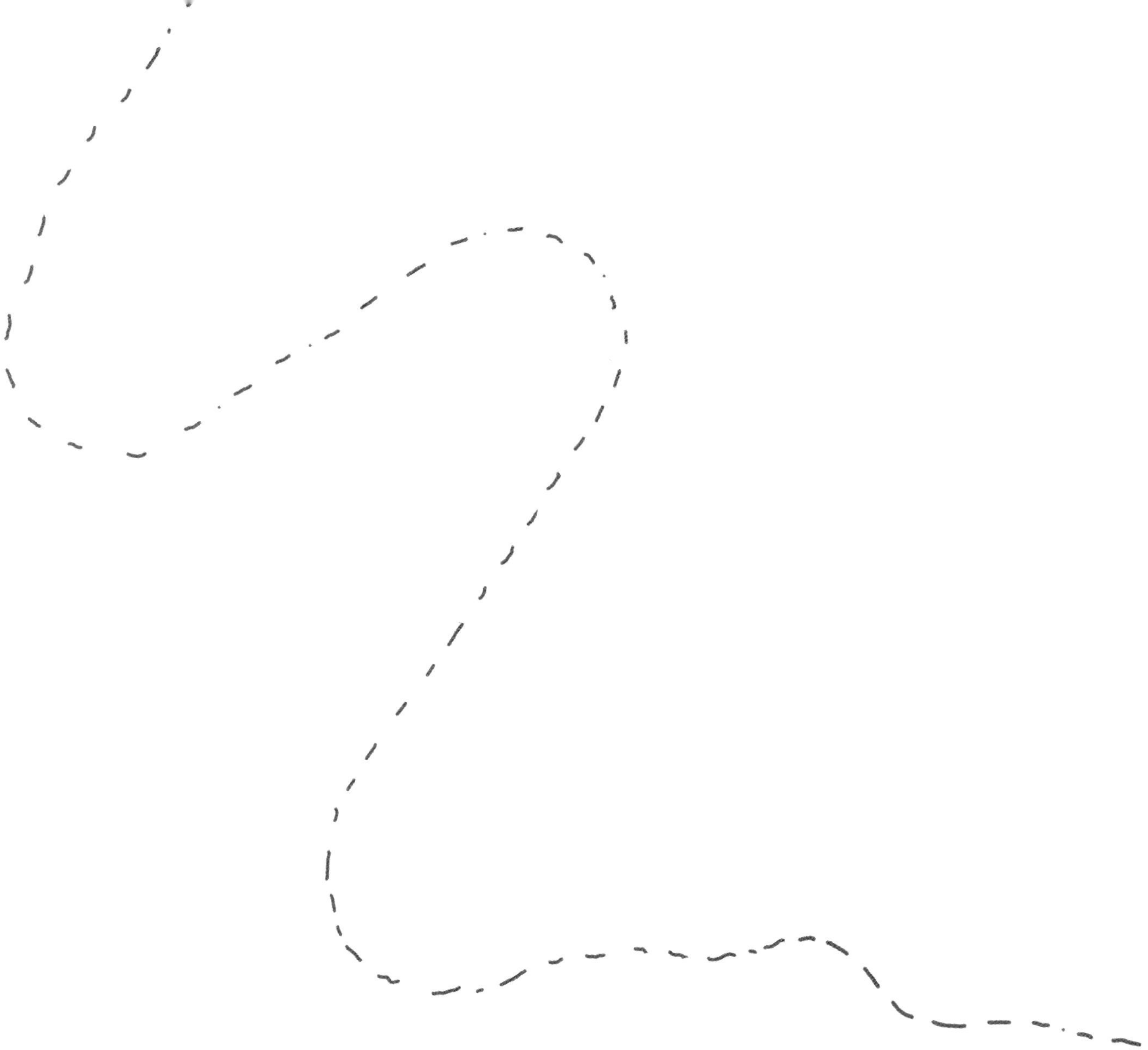

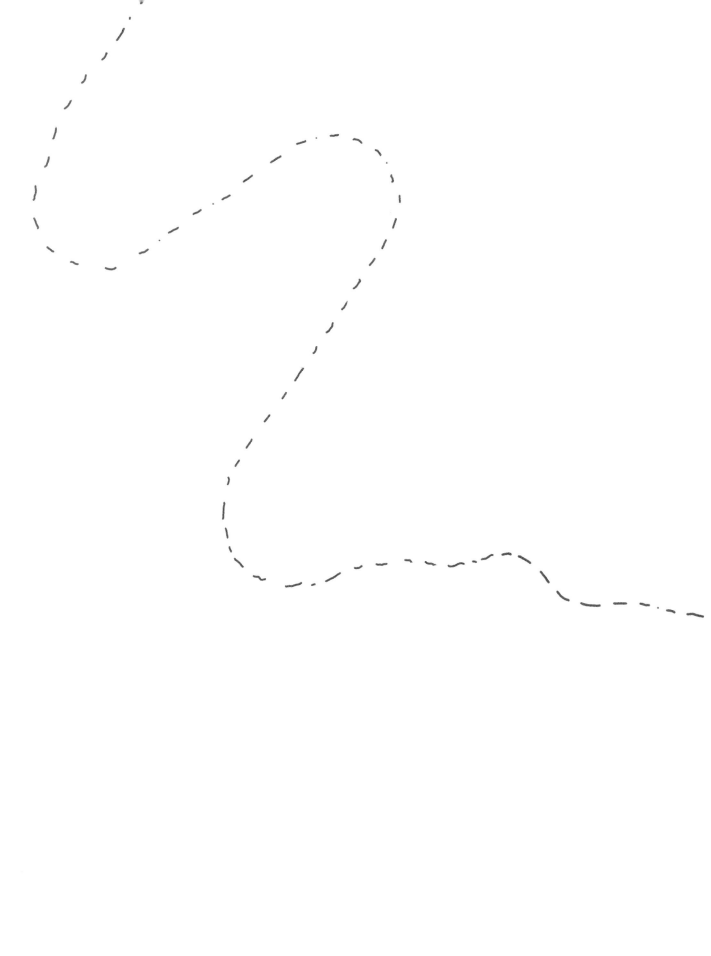

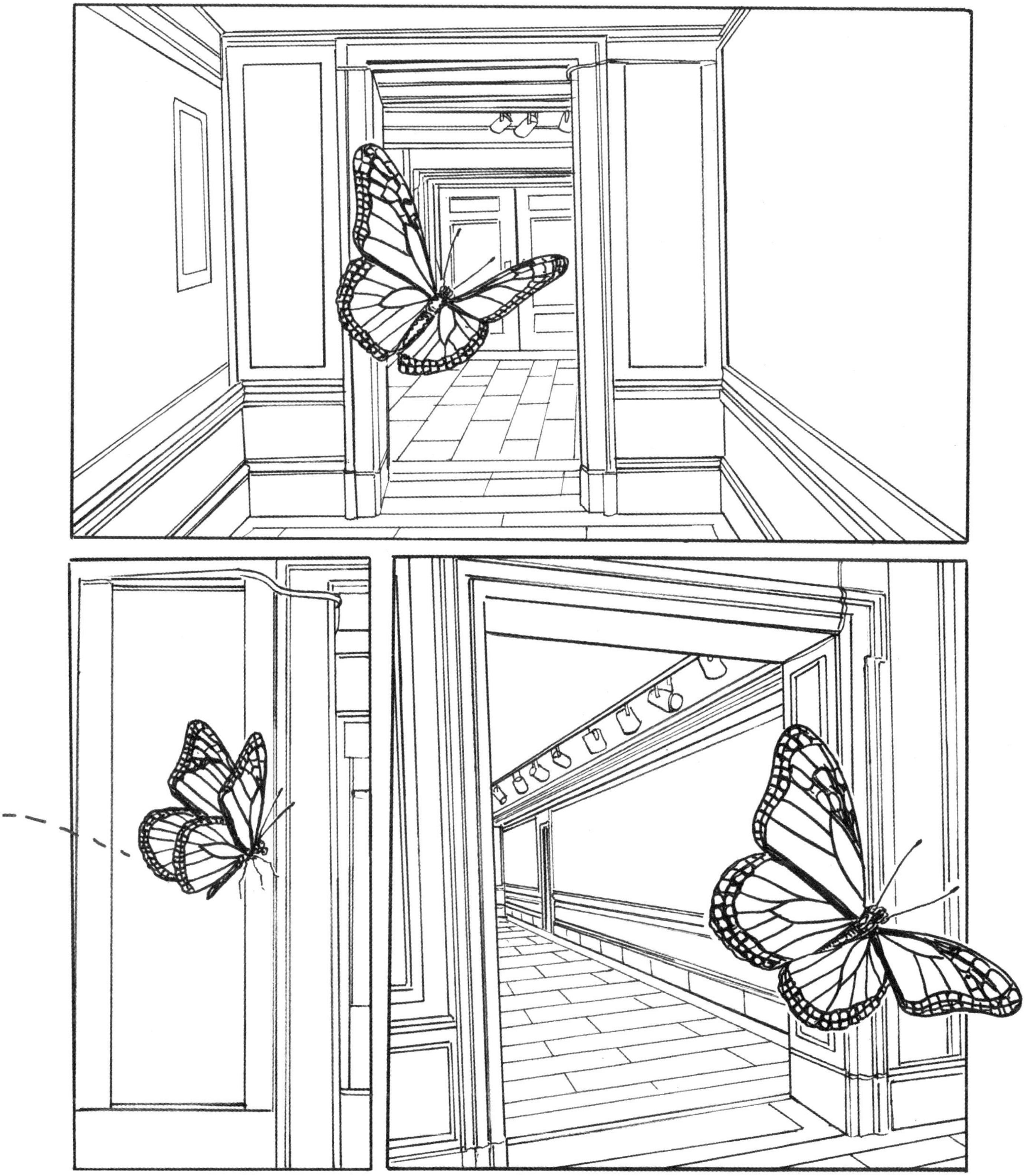

Monarch caterpillars
feed exclusively on the
milkweed plant.

Milkweed contains toxins
that make the caterpillars
unpalatable to predators.

Still, only about
five percent
survive to
adulthood.

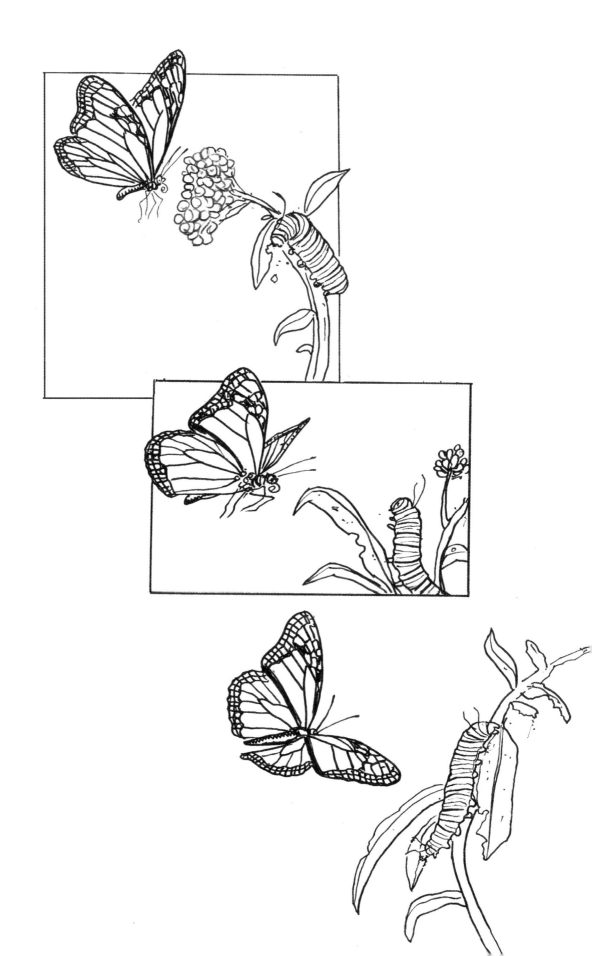

HEAR BARRETT KLEIN
TALK ABOUT DUNG BEETLES

Klein is a professor of entomology and animal
behavior and teaches cultural entomology in the
Department of Biology at the
University of Wisconsin-La Crosse.

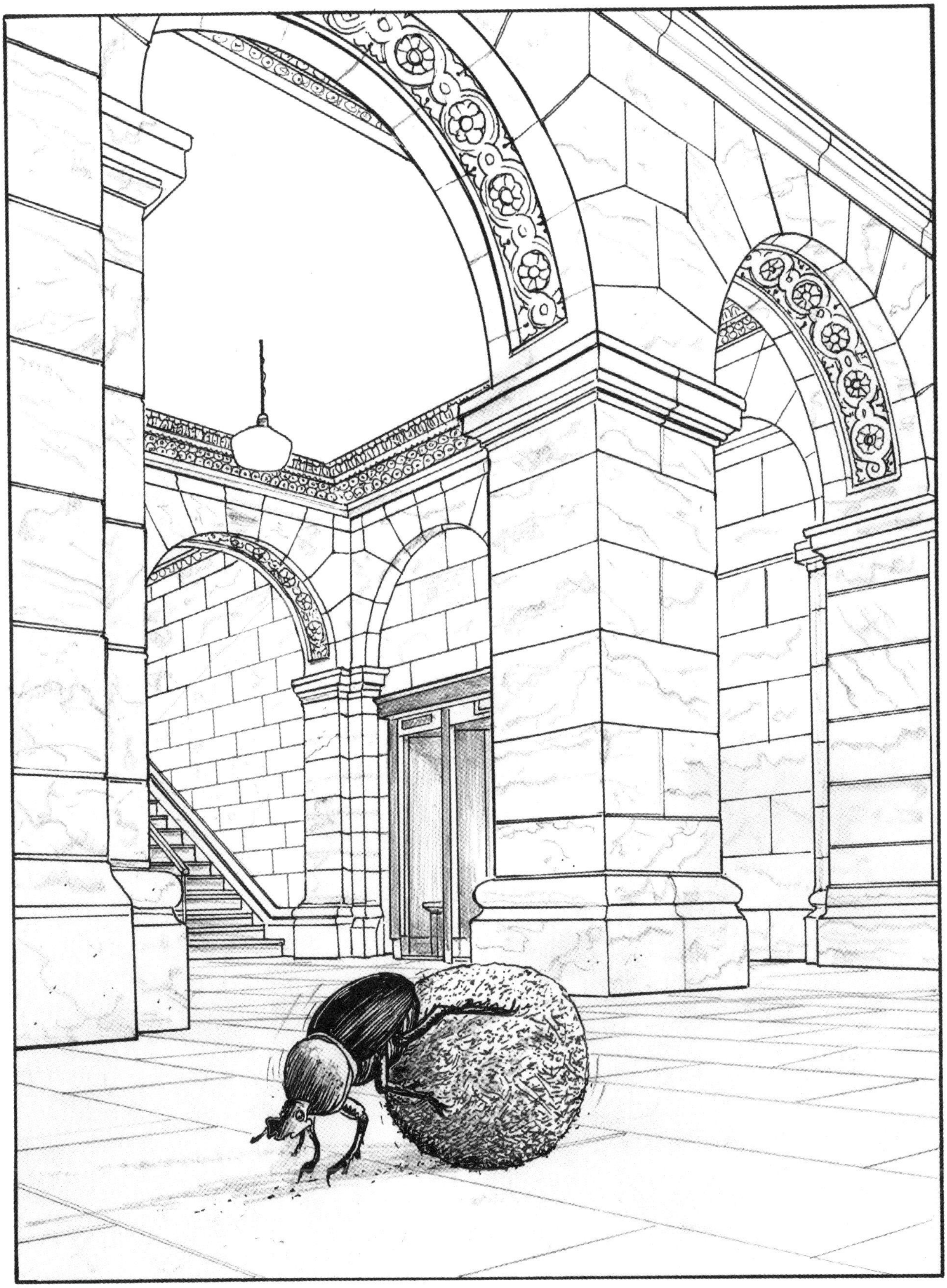

A dung beetle can
pull over **eleven
hundred**
times its own
weight —

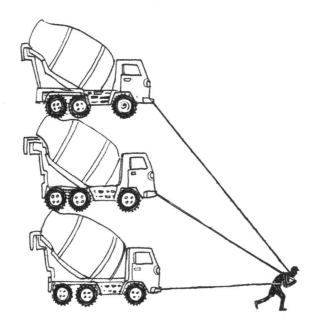

equivalent to a
human pulling three
full cement trucks.

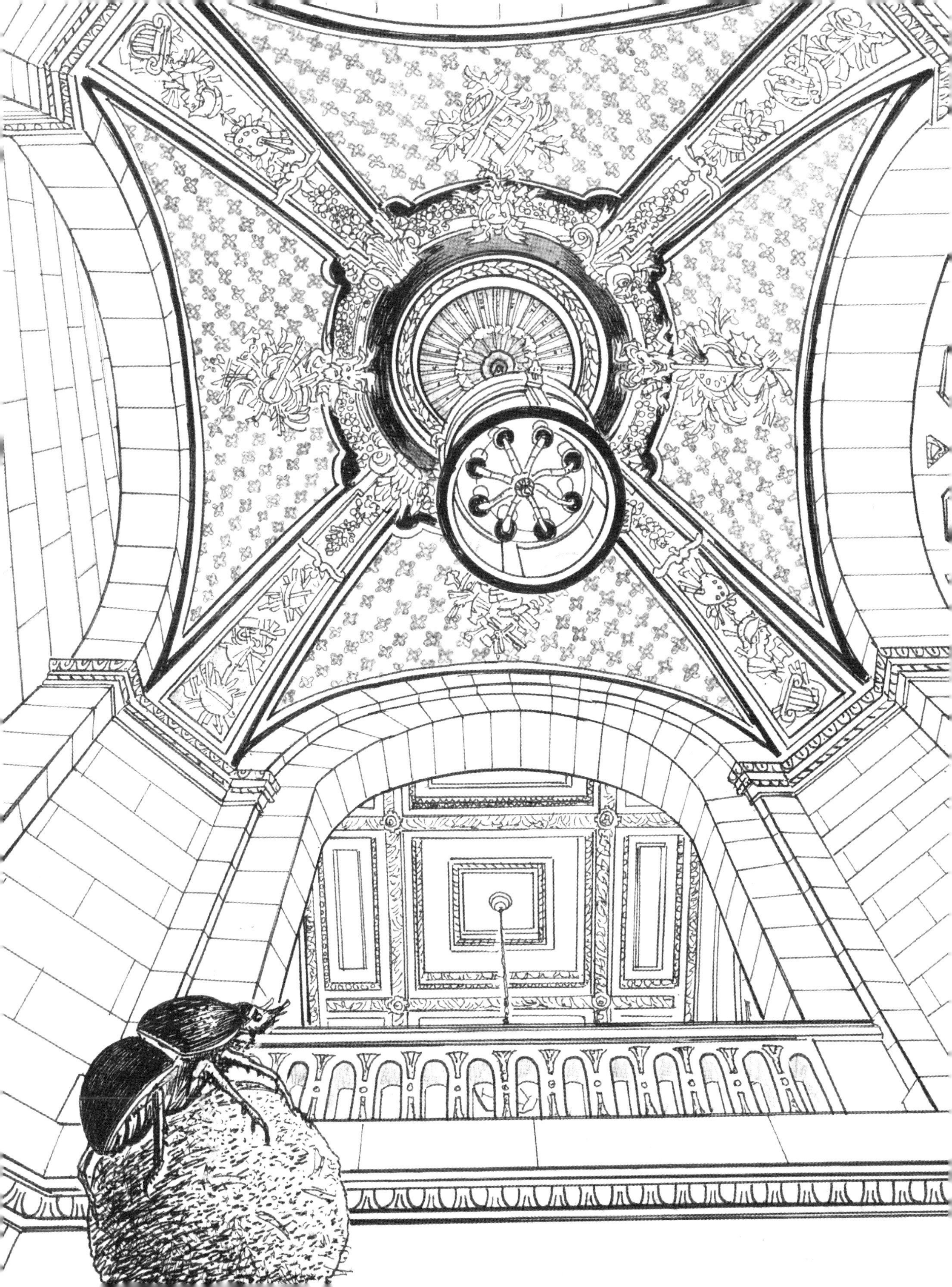

Dung beetles are the
strongest insects
in the world.

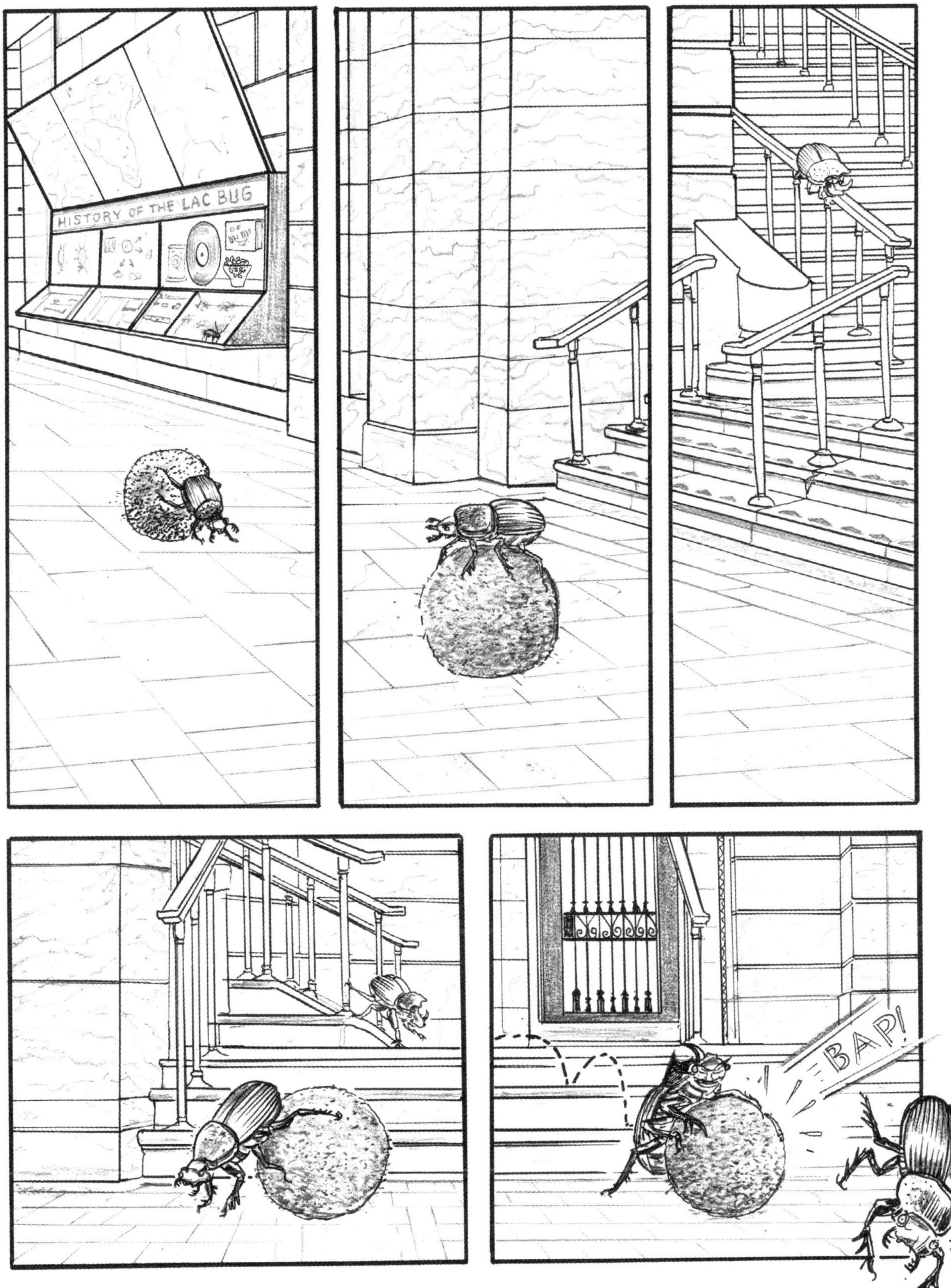
HISTORY OF THE LAC BUG
BAP!

Dung beetle walks into a bar and asks the bartender:

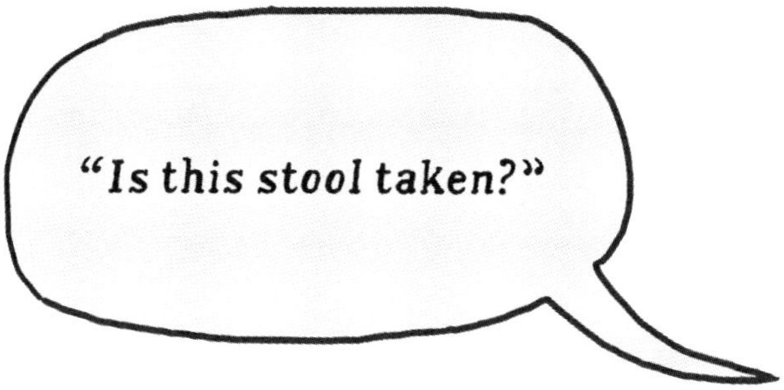
"Is this stool taken?"

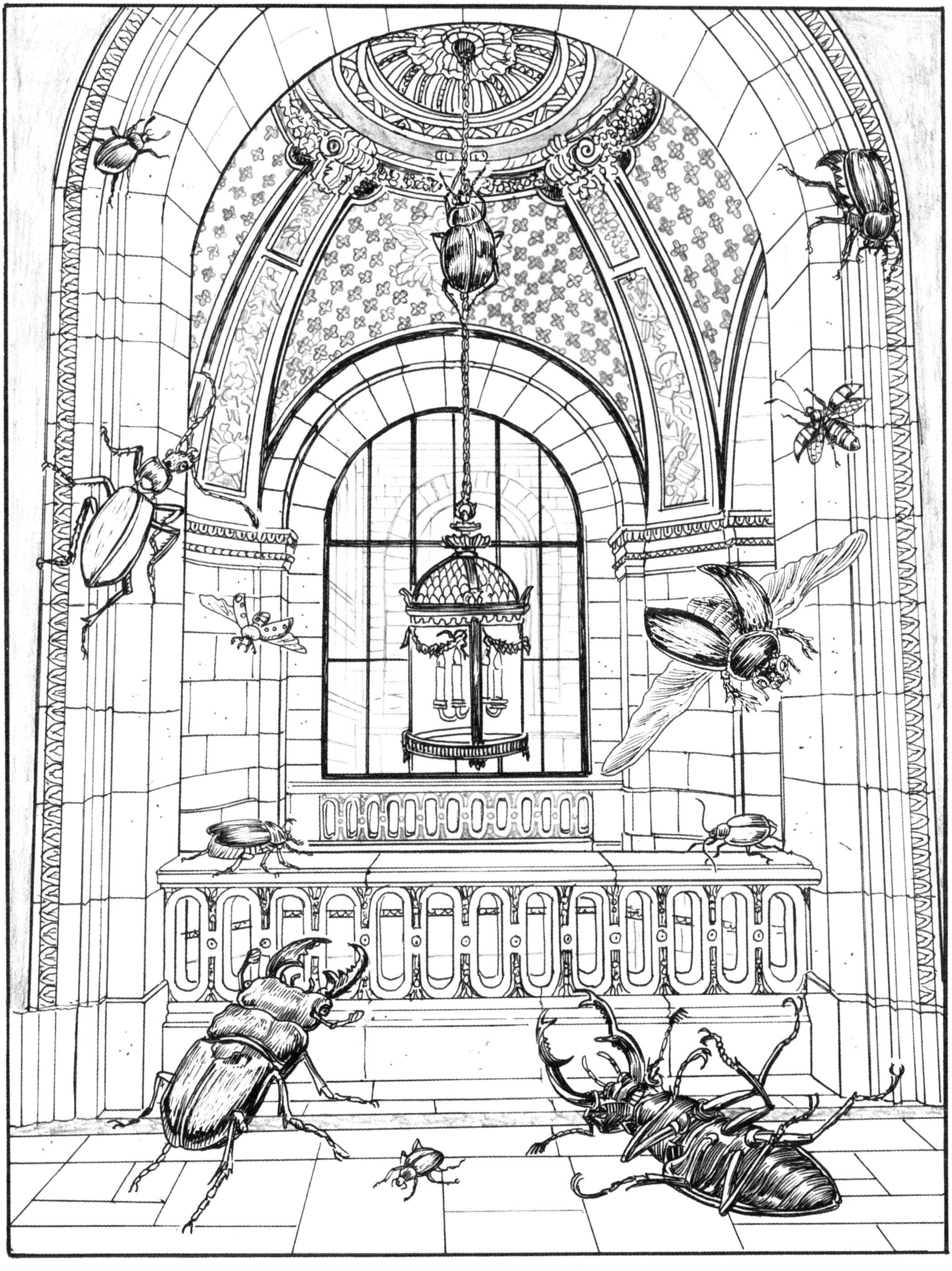

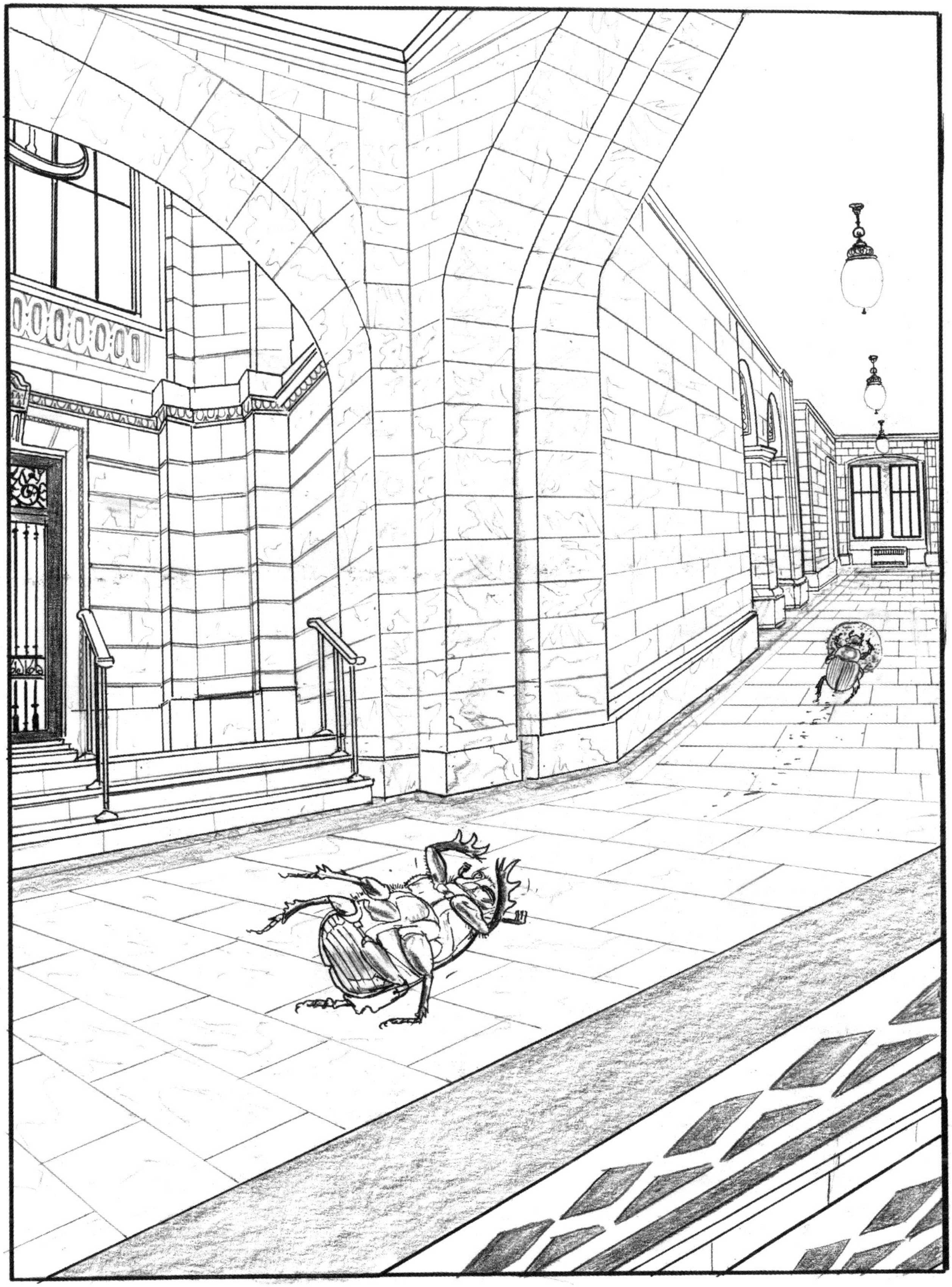

HEAR GENE KRITSKY
TALK ABOUT CICADAS

Kritsky is a professor of biology and
former chair of the Biology Department of
Mount St. Joseph University in Cincinnati, Ohio.
He cofounded the cicada resource and
tracking platform, Cicada Safari.

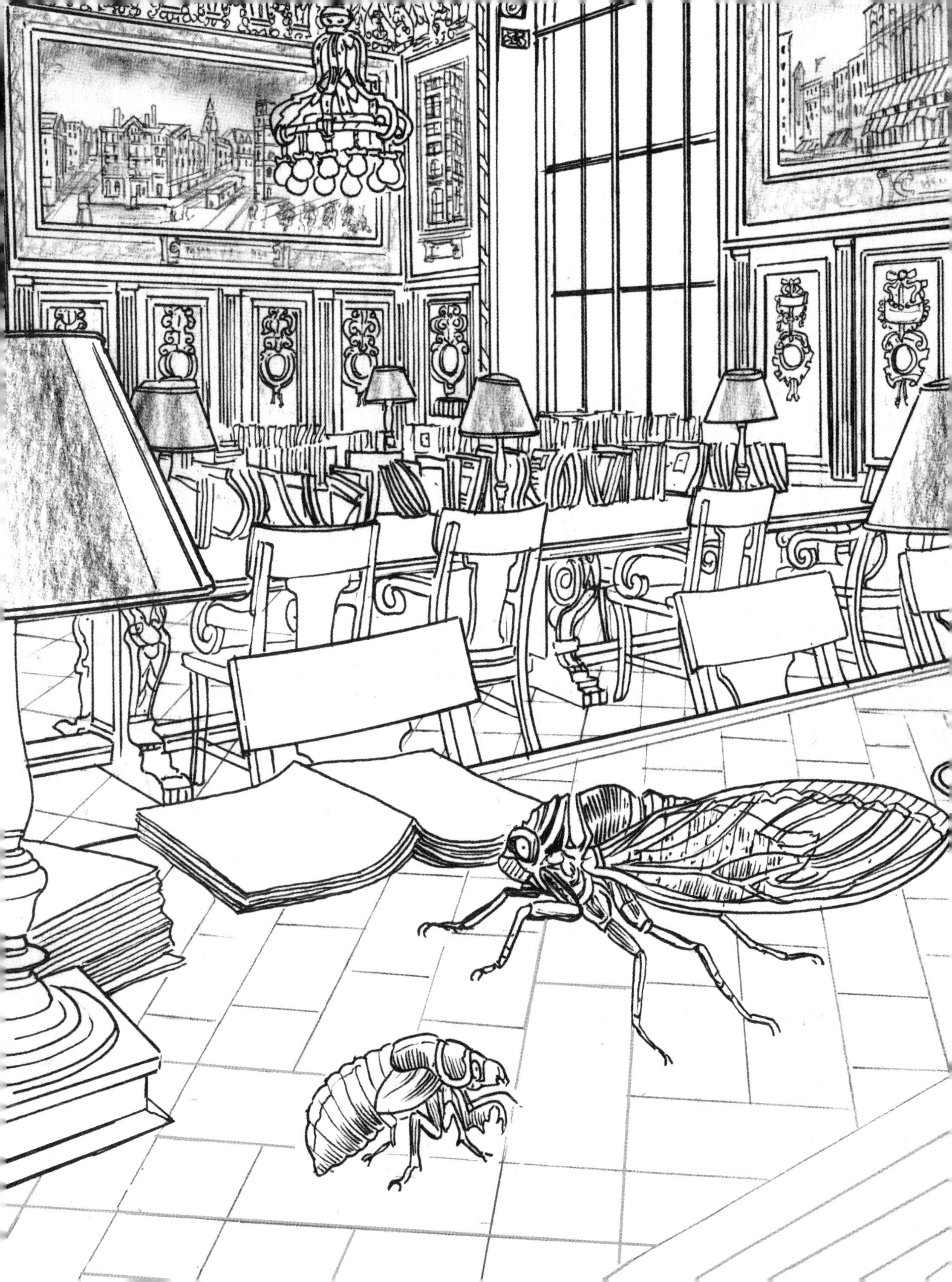

Cicadas burrow
underground and
remain there for up to
seventeen years.

They live on tree sap,
waiting for a
temperature change
that signals
them to emerge.

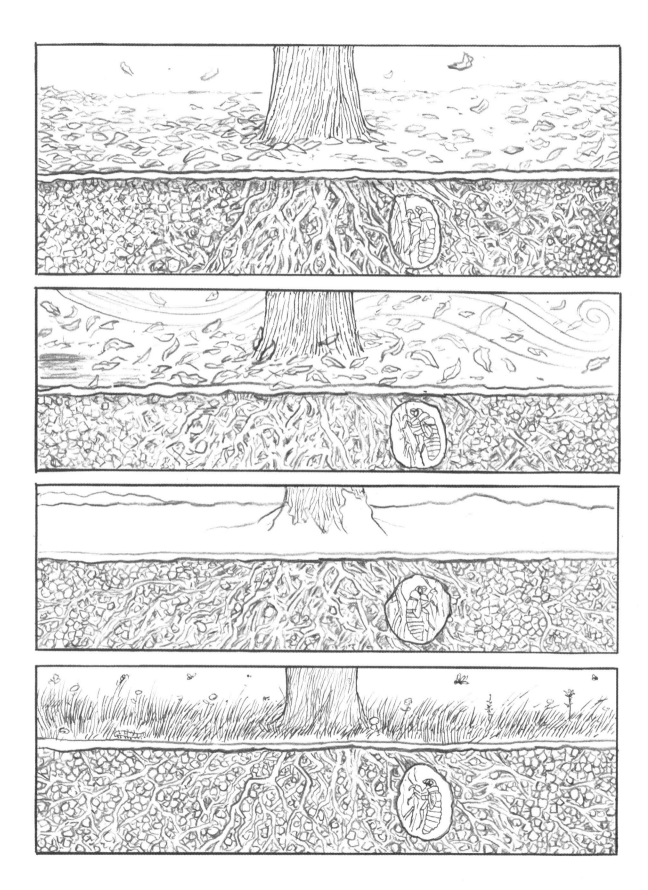

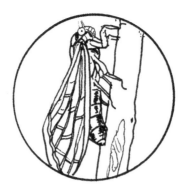

When the time comes,
they climb out of the
ground to search for a
mate and transform
into adults by the
millions.

Sometimes,
even **billions**.

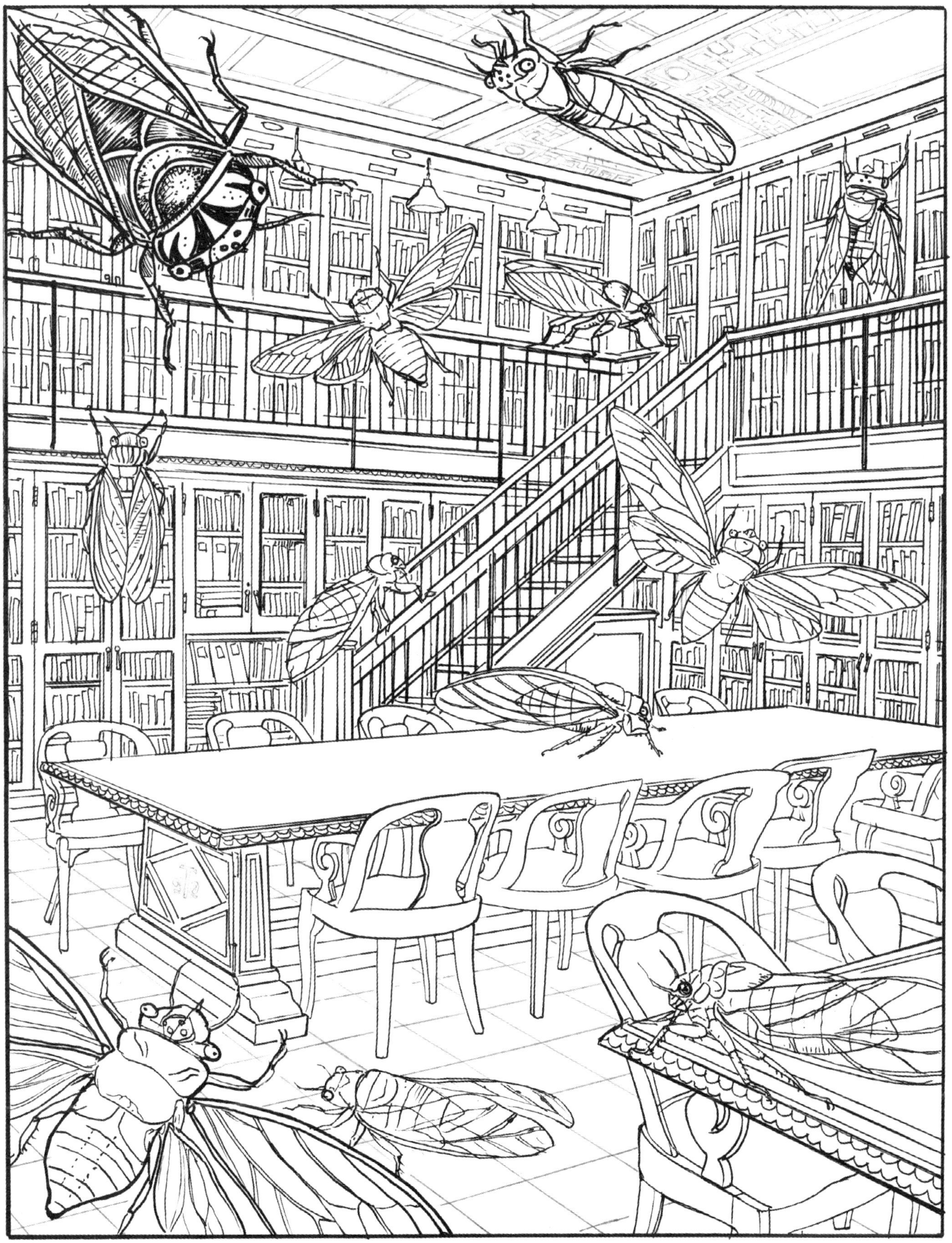

Aristotle saw cicadas
as symbols of
resurrection and
immortality.

In Plato's
Phaedrus,
Socrates
mythologized
cicadas as having once
been humans that were
enchanted by the Muses.
The Muses gave
them the ability to
sing and dance
without needing
to eat or sleep.

In Lady Murasaki Shikibu's
The Tale of Genji,
from the
eleventh century,
she wrote:
"*Where the cicada casts her shell
In the shadows of the tree,
There is one whom I love well,
Though her heart is cold to me.*"

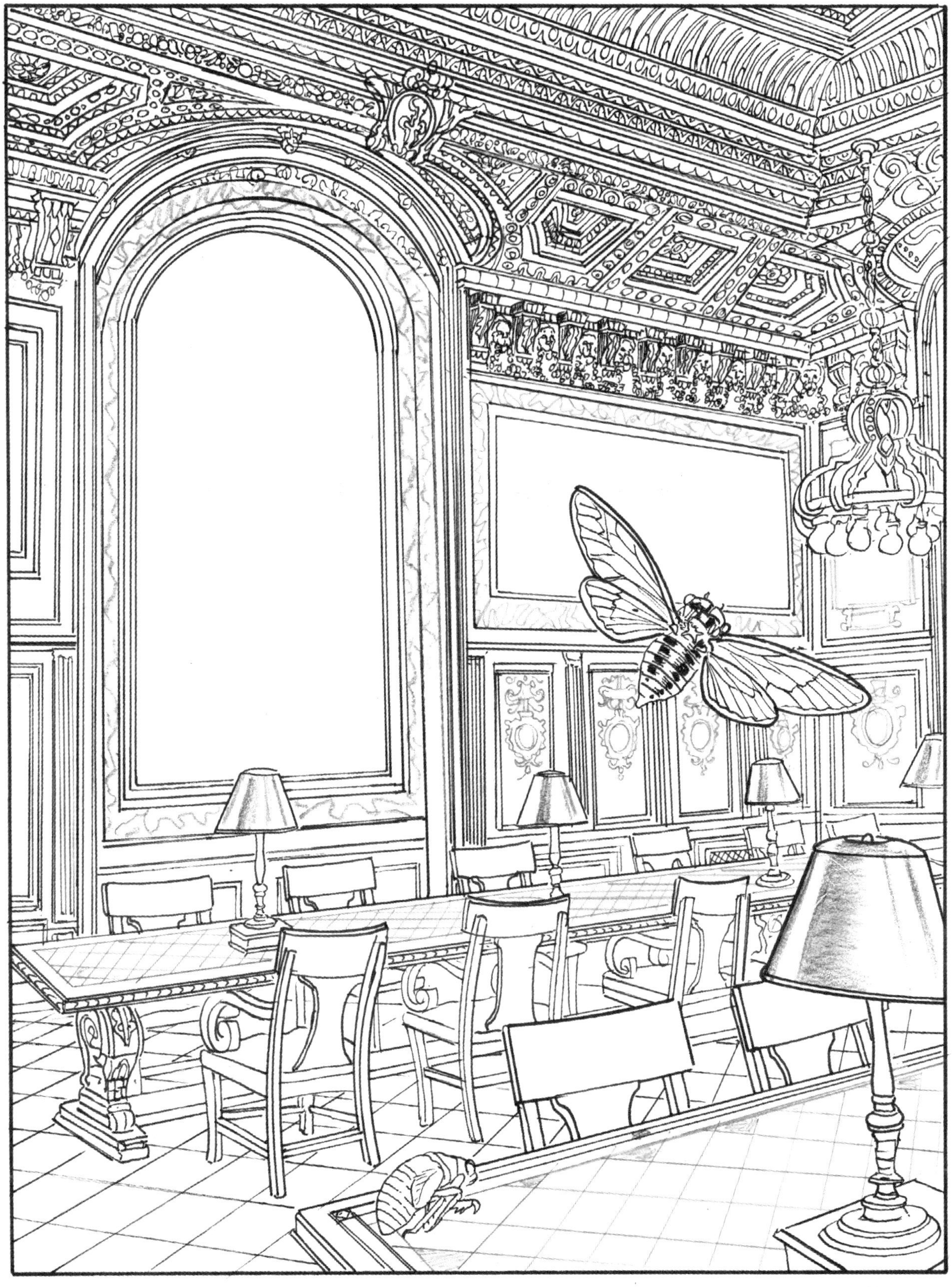

*A lot can
happen in
seventeen years.*

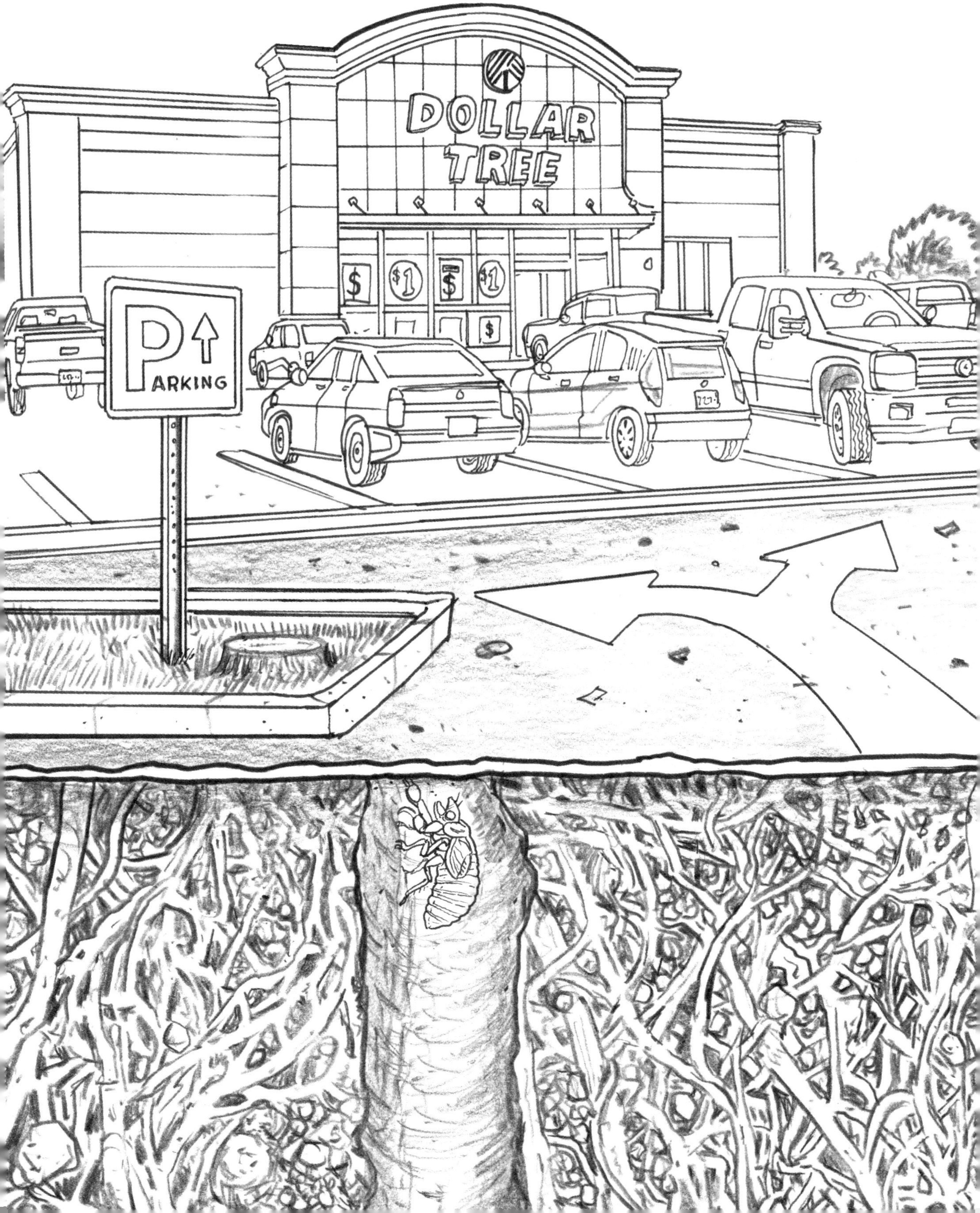
DOLLAR
TREE
$
$1
$
$1
$
PARKING

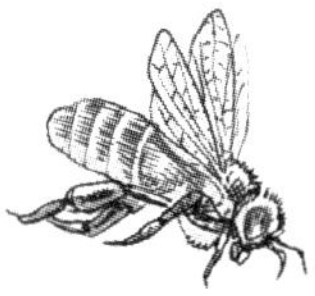

"To make a prairie it takes a clover and one bee,
One clover, and a bee,
And revery.
The revery alone will do,
If bees are few."

—Emily Dickenson
(1830–1886)
from
The Poems of Emily Dickinson

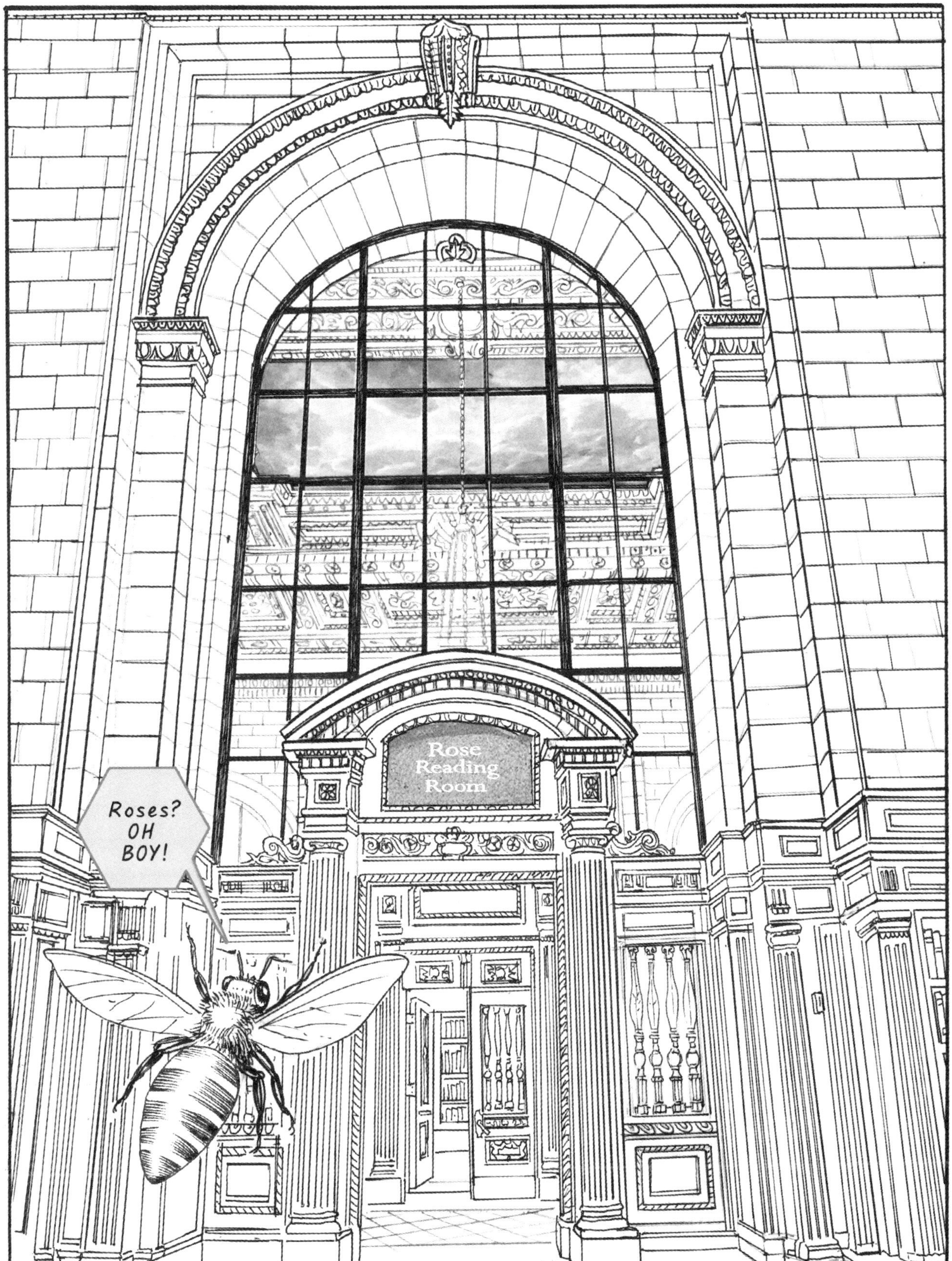
Rose Reading Room
Roses? OH BOY!

HEAR MICHAEL S. ENGEL
TALK ABOUT BEES

Engel is a paleontologist and entomologist.
He was a distinguished professor of
ecology and evolutionary biology at the
University of Kansas and a senior
curator at the university's Biodiversity
Institute and Natural History Museum.

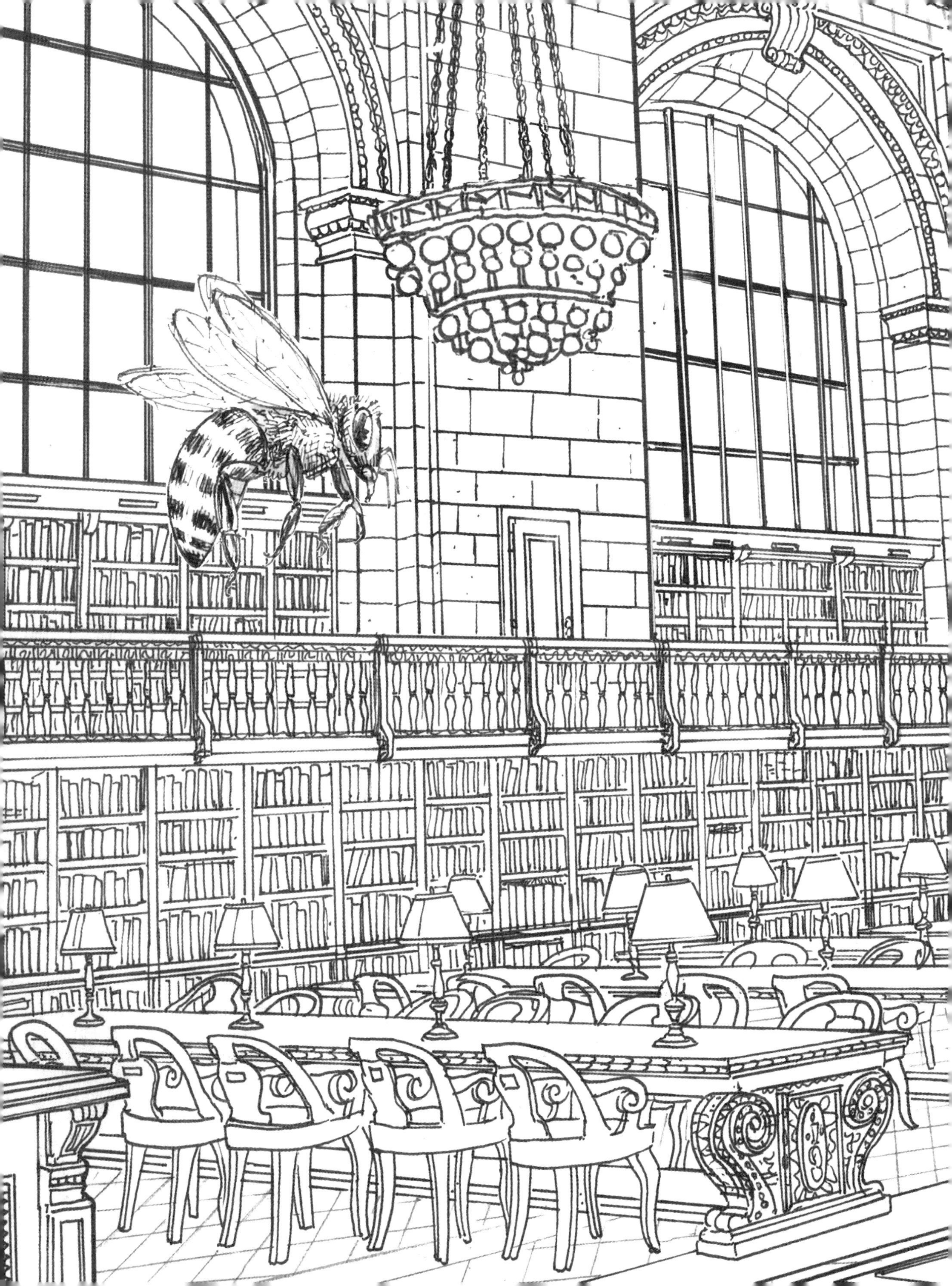

Honey bees perform a "waggle dance"
that allows them to communicate the
exact location of food sources to
members of the nest.

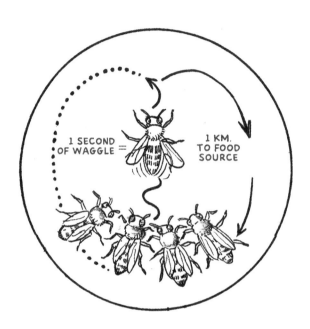

1 SECOND
OF WAGGLE =

1 KM.
TO FOOD
SOURCE

This complex dance pattern communicates
the direction and distance to the food
relative to the sun's position in the sky.

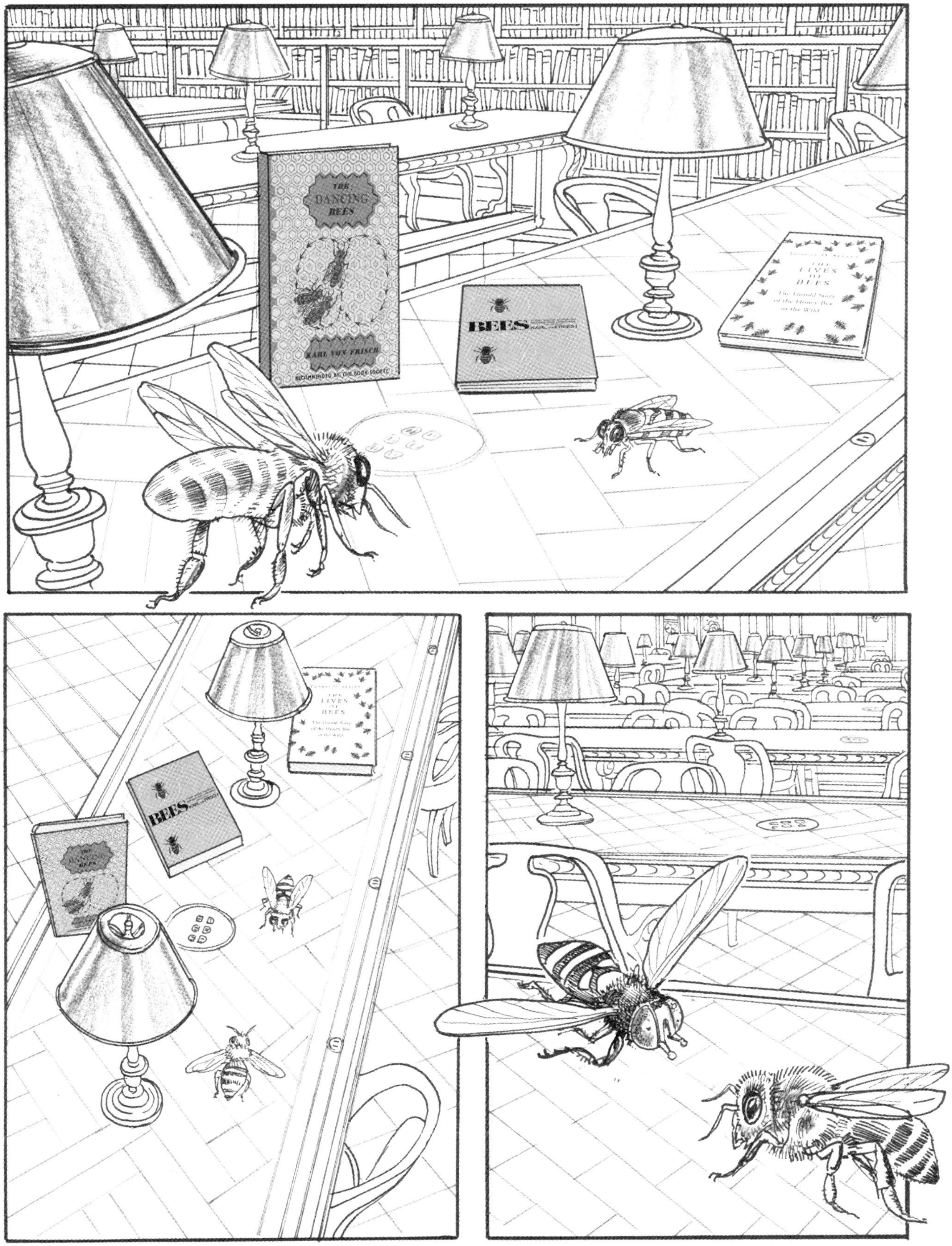
THE DANCING BEES
KARL VON FRISCH
RECOMMENDED BY THE BOOK SOCIETY
BEES
KARL VON FRISCH
THE LIVES OF BEES
The Untold Story of the Honey Bee in the Wild

"Bee! I'm expecting you!
Was saying Yesterday
To Somebody you know
That you were due—

The Frogs got Home last Week—
Are settled, and at work—
Birds, mostly back—
The Clover warm and thick—

You'll get my Letter by
The seventeeth; Reply
Or better, be with me—
Yours, Fly."

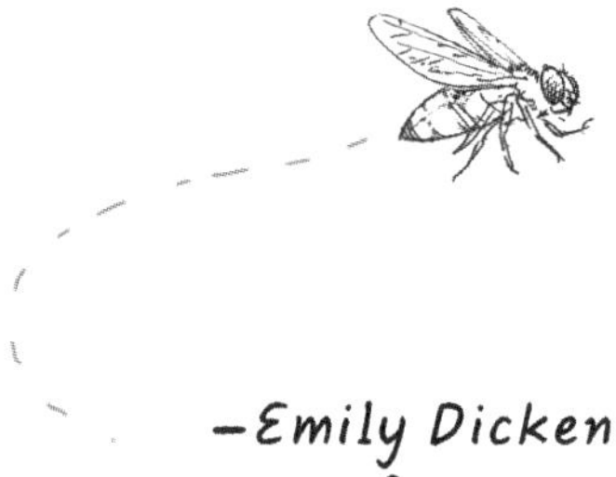

—Emily Dickenson
from
The Poems of
Emily Dickinson

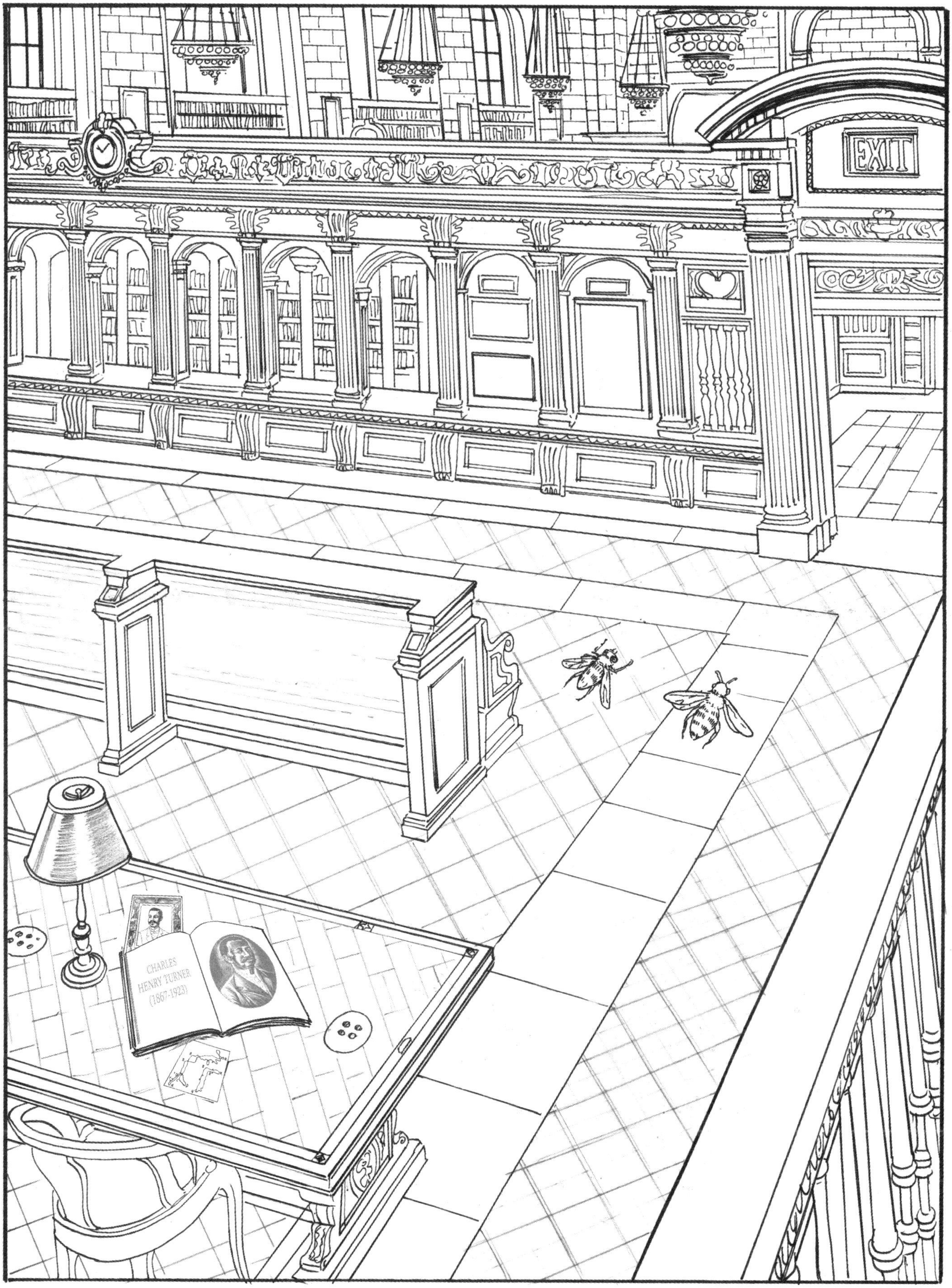
EXIT
CHARLES
HENRY TURNER
(1867-1923)

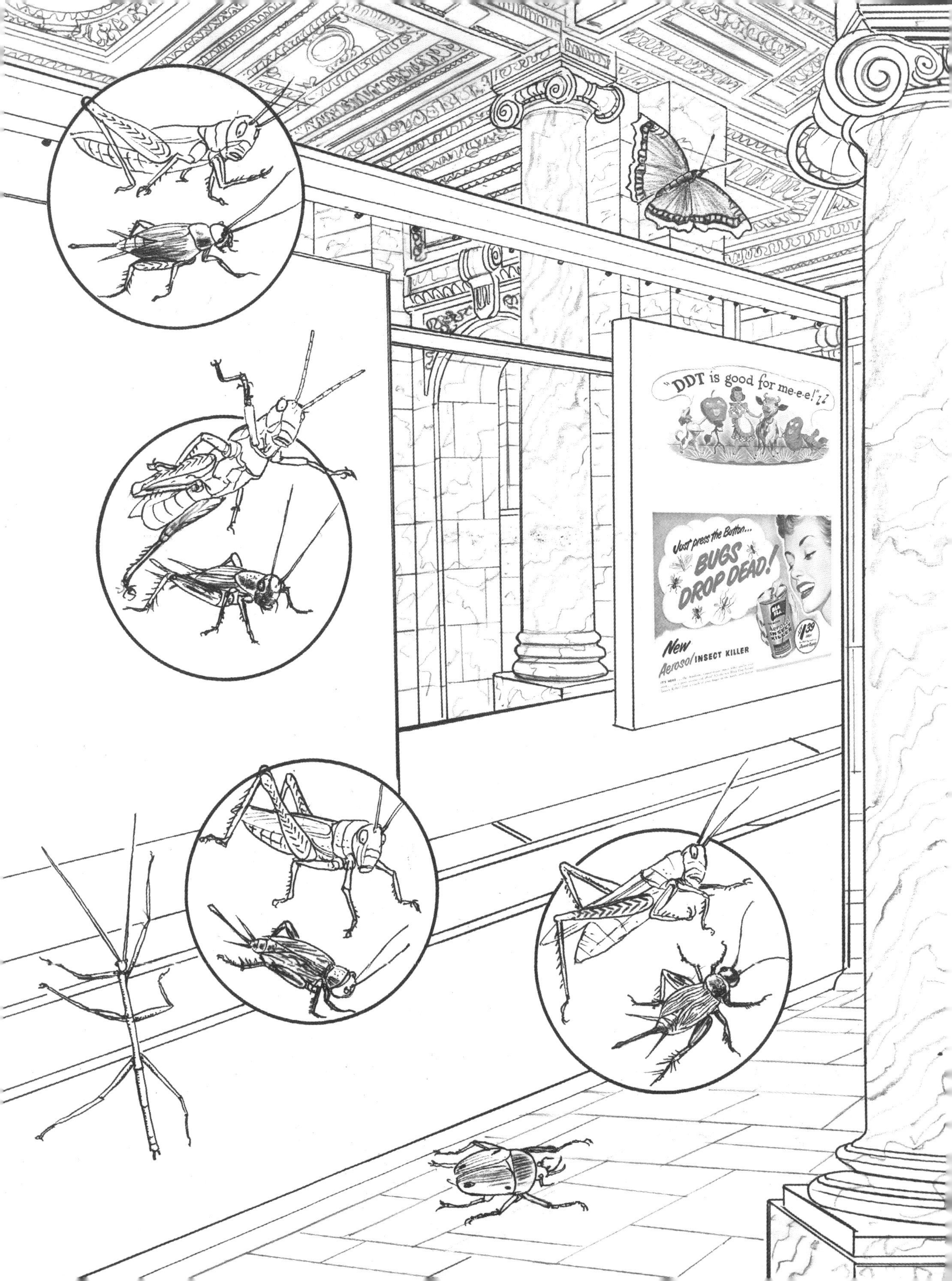
"DDT is good for me-e-e!"
Just press the Button...
BUGS DROP DEAD!
New
Aerosol INSECT KILLER

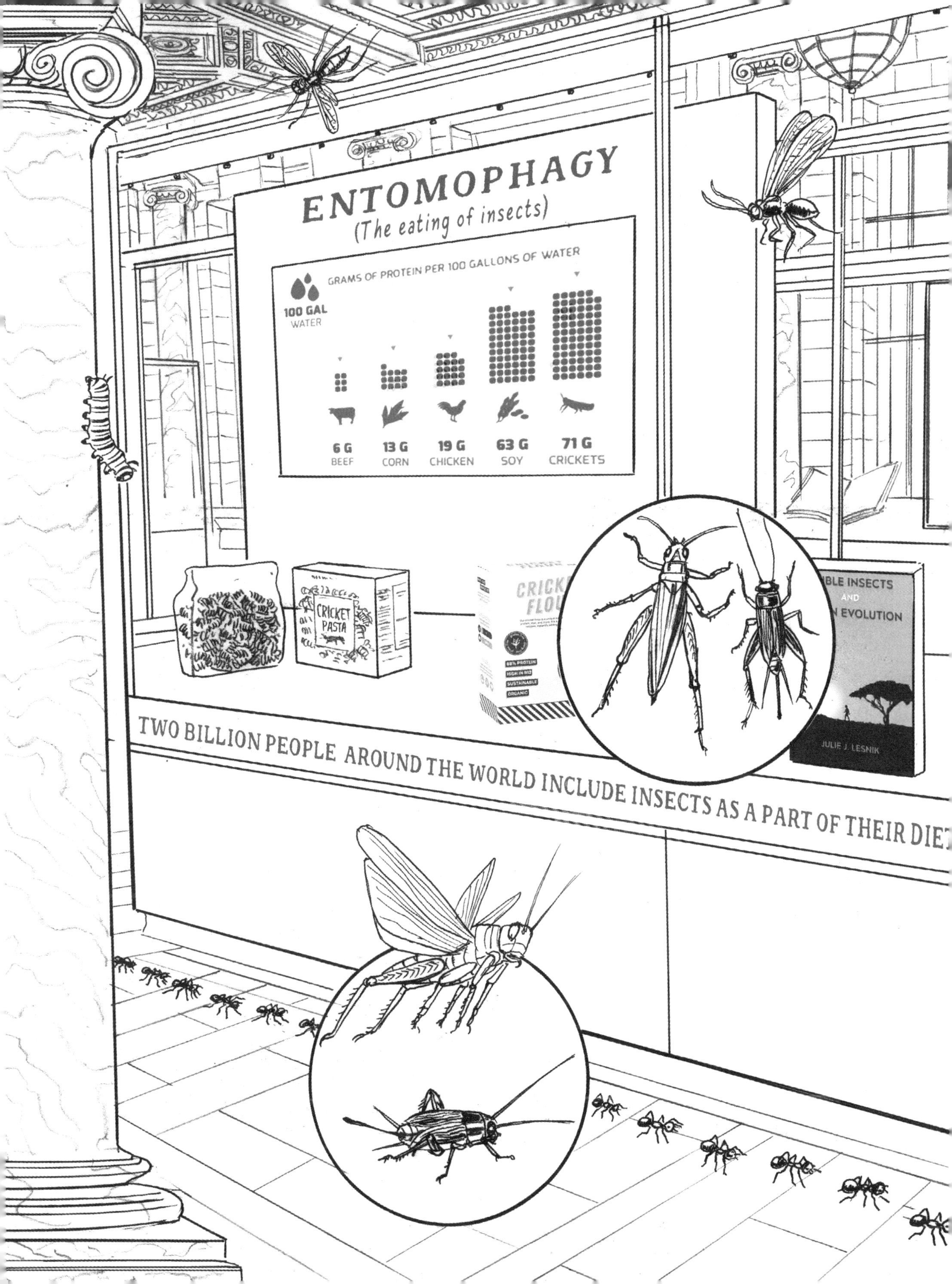

ENTOMOPHAGY
(The eating of insects)
GRAMS OF PROTEIN PER 100 GALLONS OF WATER
100 GAL
WATER
6 G
BEEF
13 G
CORN
19 G
CHICKEN
63 G
SOY
71 G
CRICKETS
CRICKET
PASTA
68% PROTEIN
HIGH IN B12
SUSTAINABLE
ORGANIC
BLE INSECTS
AND
N EVOLUTION
JULIE J. LESNIK
TWO BILLION PEOPLE AROUND THE WORLD INCLUDE INSECTS AS A PART OF THEIR DIET

HEAR JESSICA LEE WARE TALK ABOUT DRAGONFLIES

Ware is an evolutionary biologist and entomologist. She is an associate curator of Odonata (dragonflies and damselflies) and non-Holometabolous Minor Orders at the American Museum of Natural History.

Dragonfly

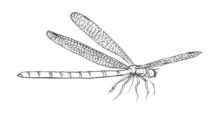

Damselfly

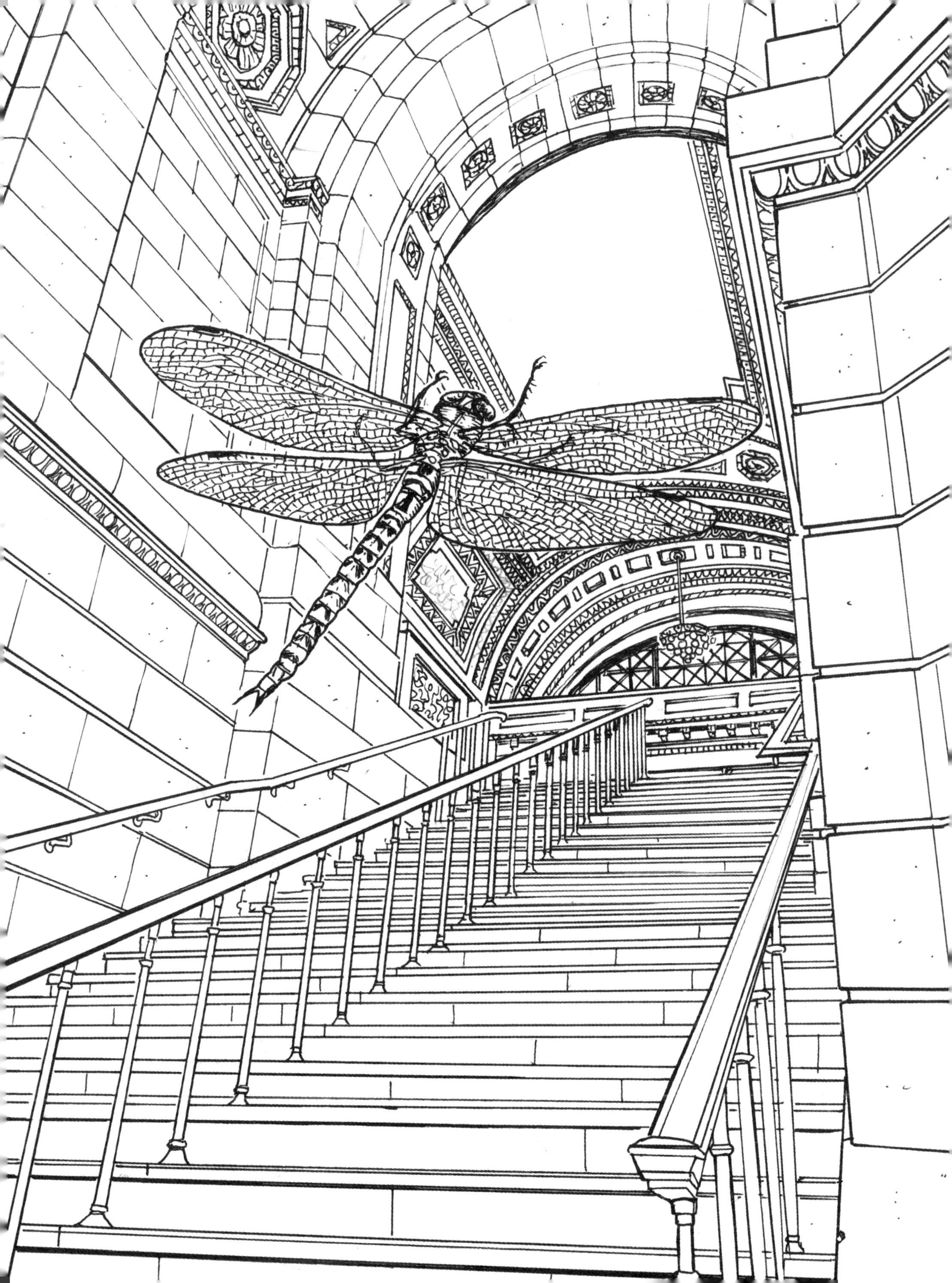

In eighteenth-century
Japan, samurai
wore helmets with
dragonfly motifs.

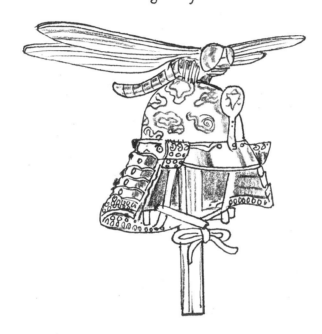

They called dragonflies
kachi-mushi—
"victorious insect"—
symbolizing prowess,
agility, and determination
in battle.

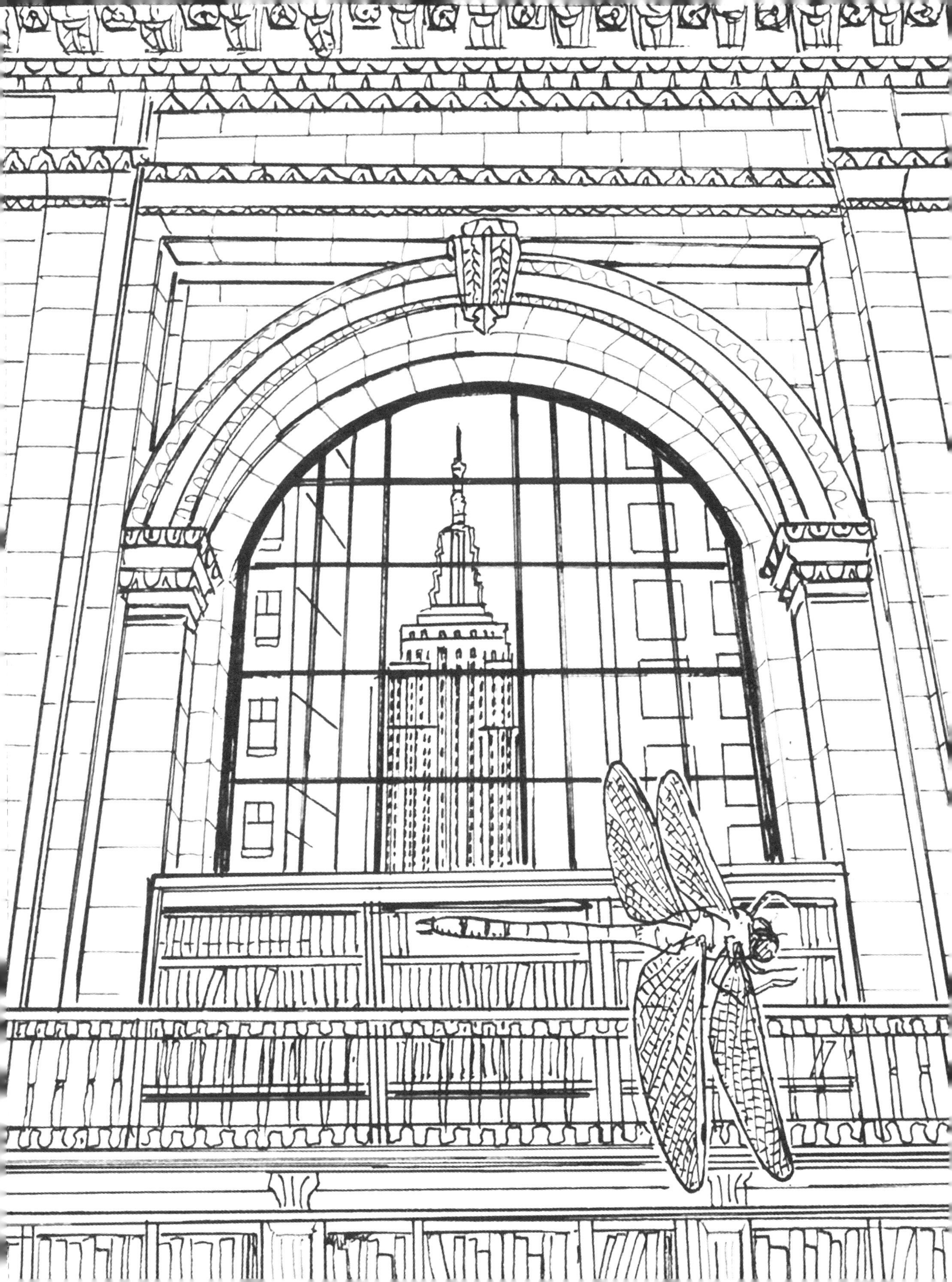

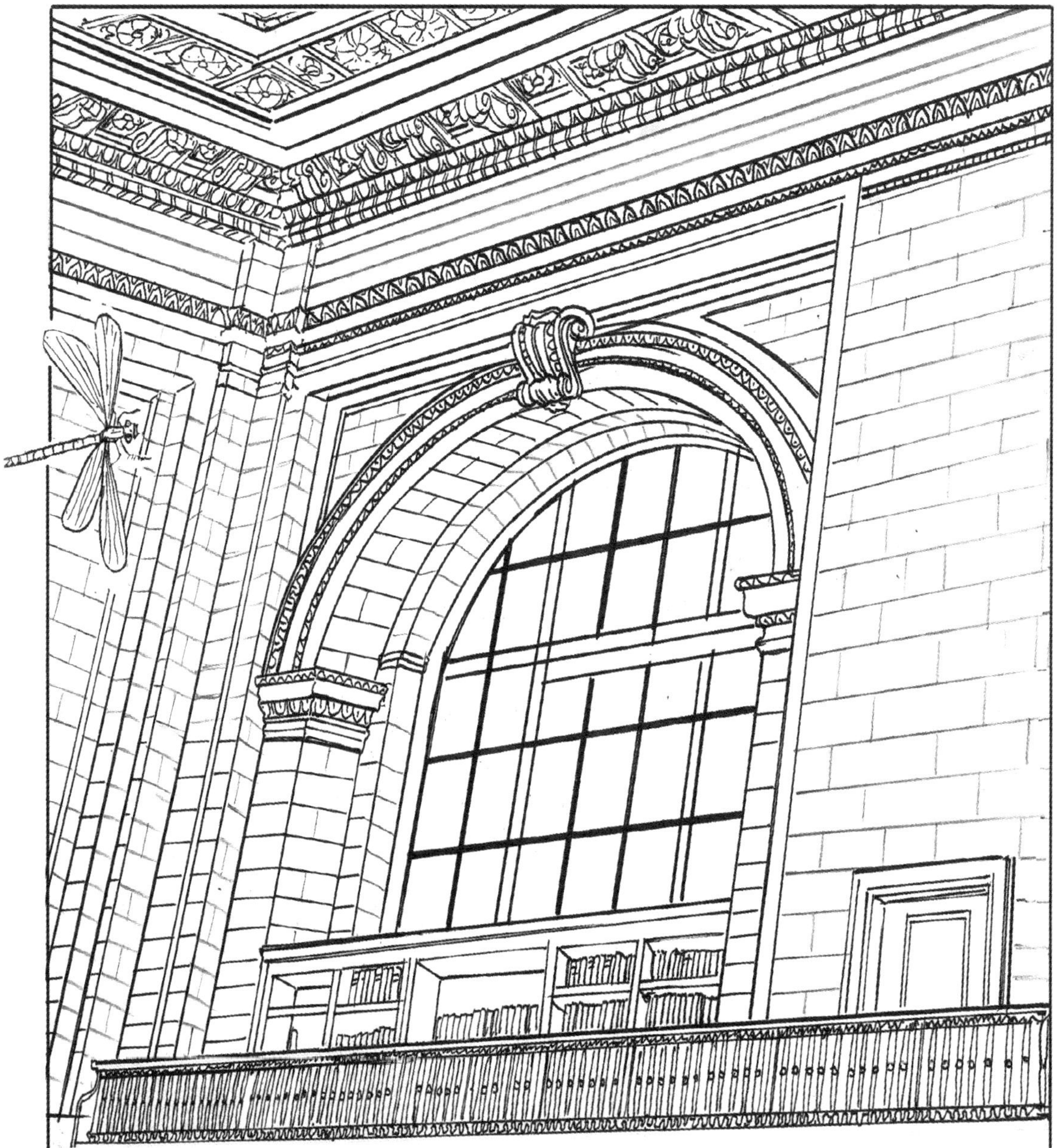

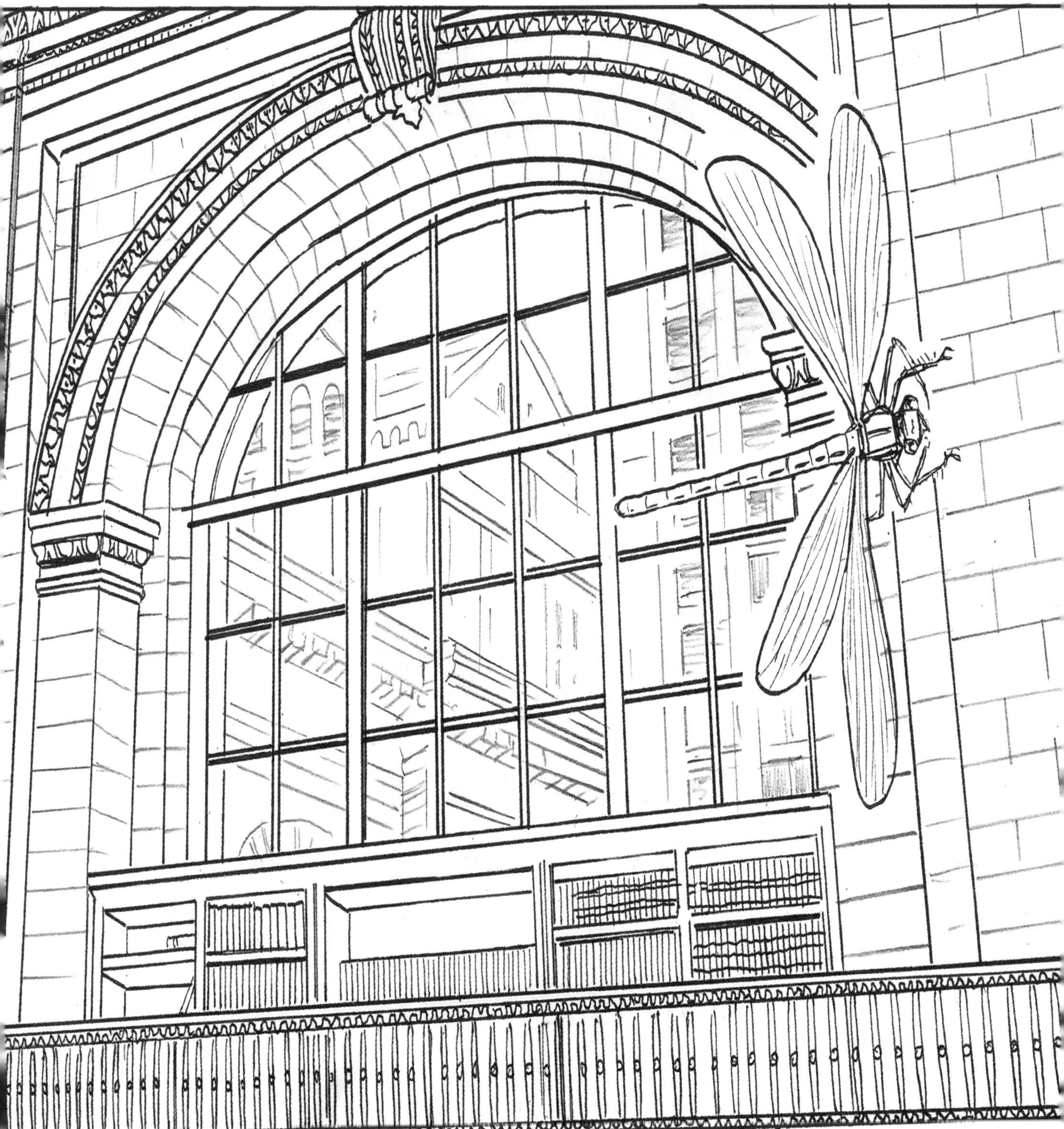

The Chinese
believed a dragonfly
entering their home
was good luck. It meant
something positive was
about to happen.

Buddhists
connected dragonflies
with life's innermost
truths—the noble path
to attain true wisdom.

Some Native
Americans, like the
Hopi Tribe, thought
of them as healers and
associated them with
pure water and
swiftness.

Because of their pointy
tails, some people called
them "The Devil's darning
needle."

Or just
"The Devil!"

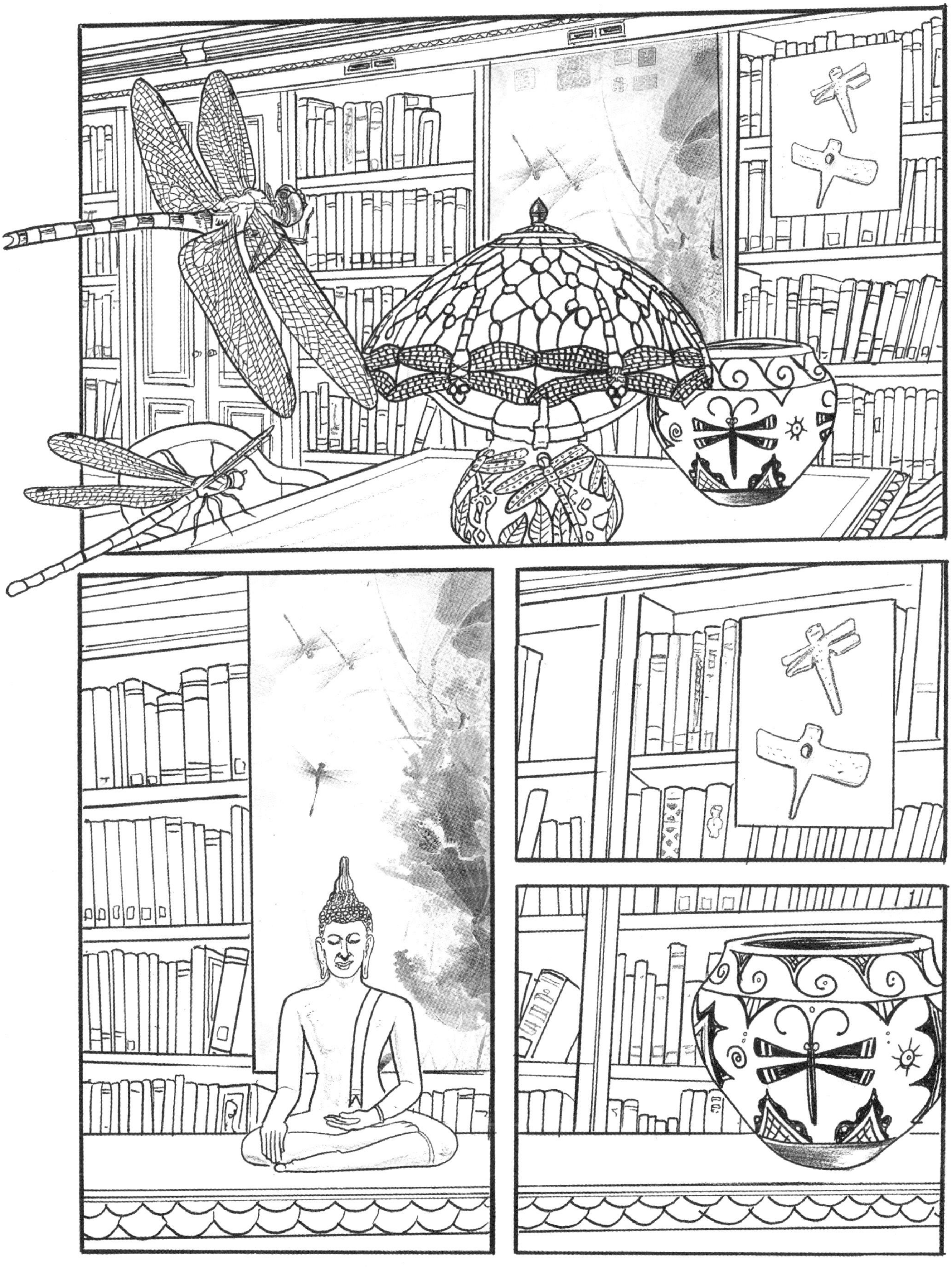

Margaret S. Collins
(1922–1996)

She was a child prodogy, civil rights activist,
and the first African American woman
to earn a PhD in entomology.

She specialized in the study of termites.

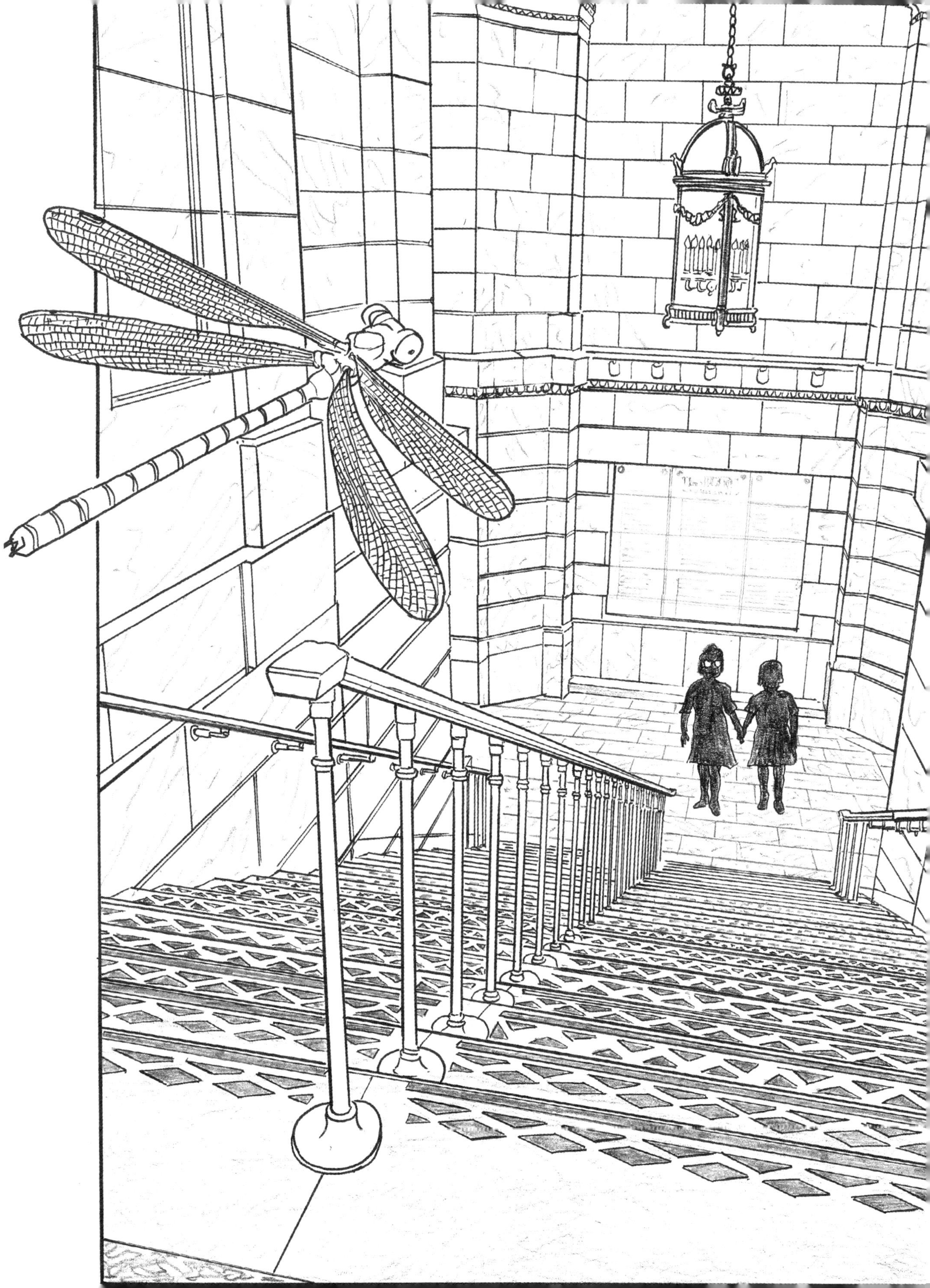

Rachel Carson
(1907–1964)
She is considered to be the author
of the environmental movement.

Her landmark book, *Silent Spring*,
made the public aware of the
devastating impact pesticides
were having on the entire eco-
system and led to policy changes.

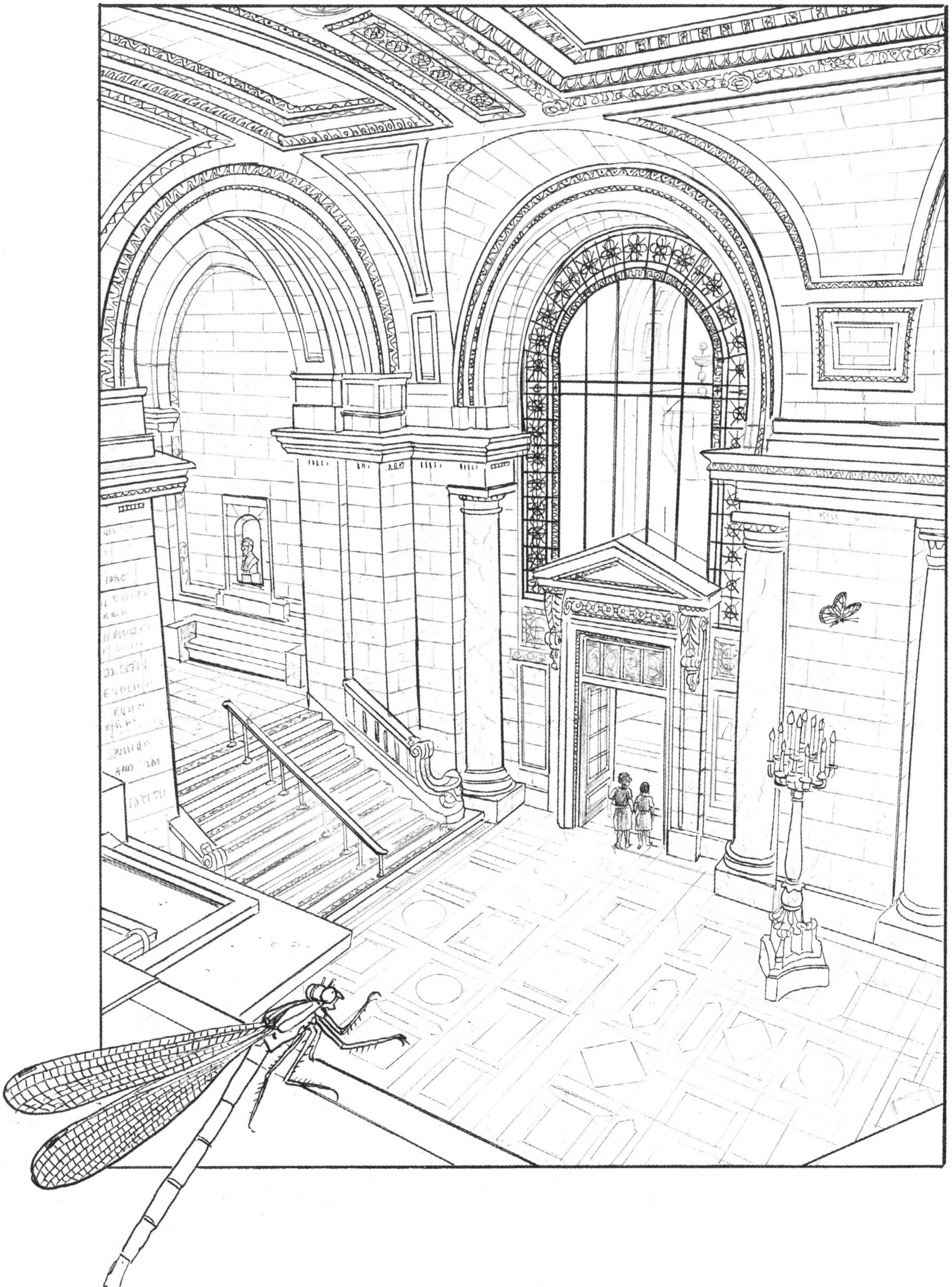

HEAR MARK W. MOFFETT
TALK ABOUT ANTS

Moffett is an ecologist and explorer who
has been called the Indiana Jones of entomology.
He is a biologist who studies the ecology of
tropical forest canopies and the social
behavior of animals and humans.

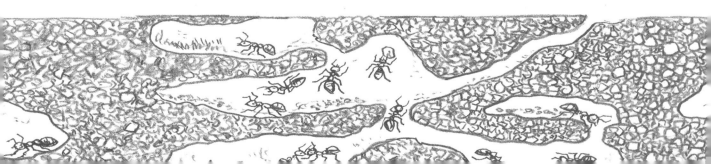

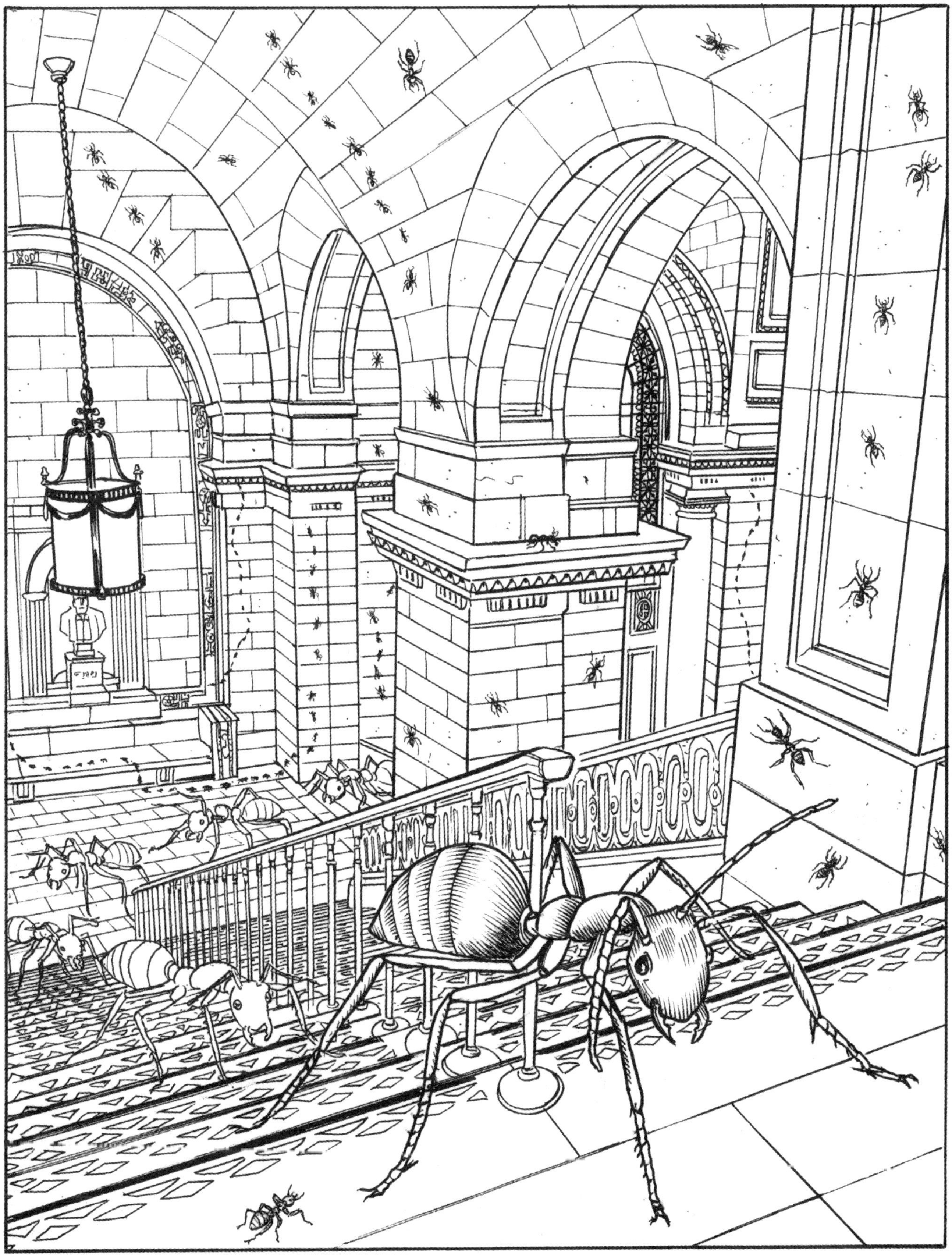

"Nature will bear the closest inspection.
She invites us to lay our eye level
with her smallest leaf, and take an
insect view of its plain."

— Henry David Thoreau
(1817-1862)
from his journals

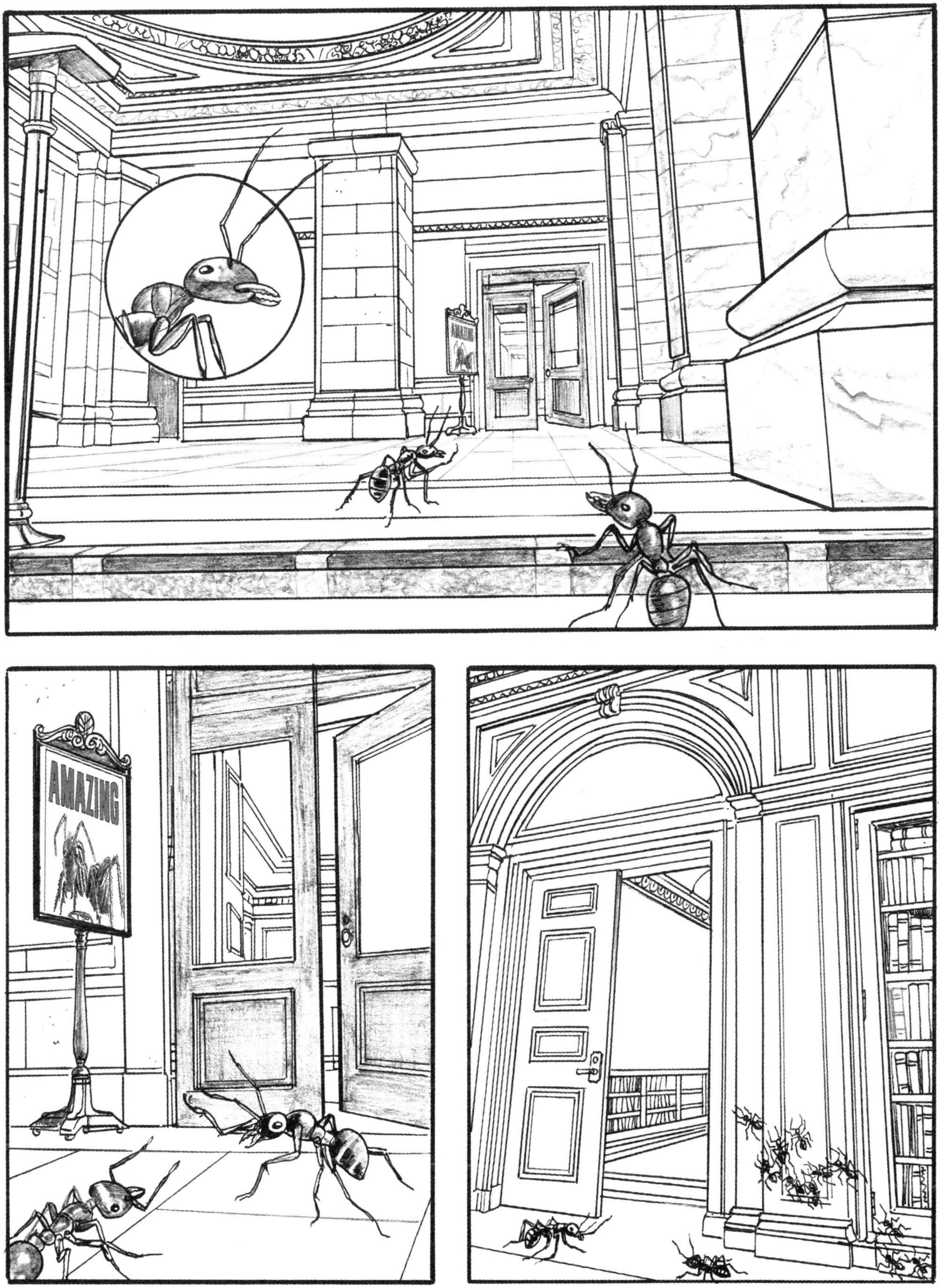
AMAZING
AMAZING

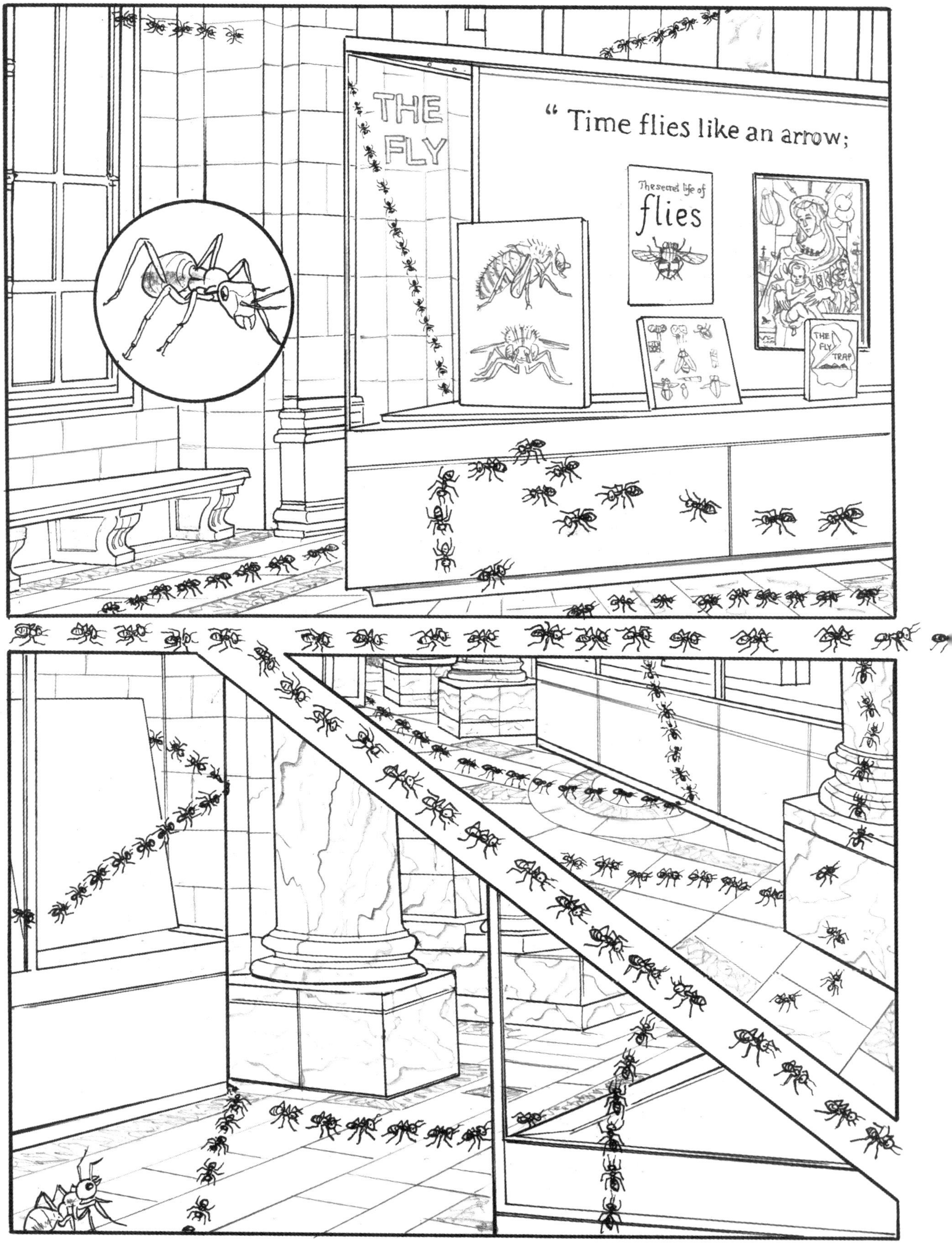
THE FLY
“ Time flies like an arrow;
The secret life of
flies
THE FLY TRAP

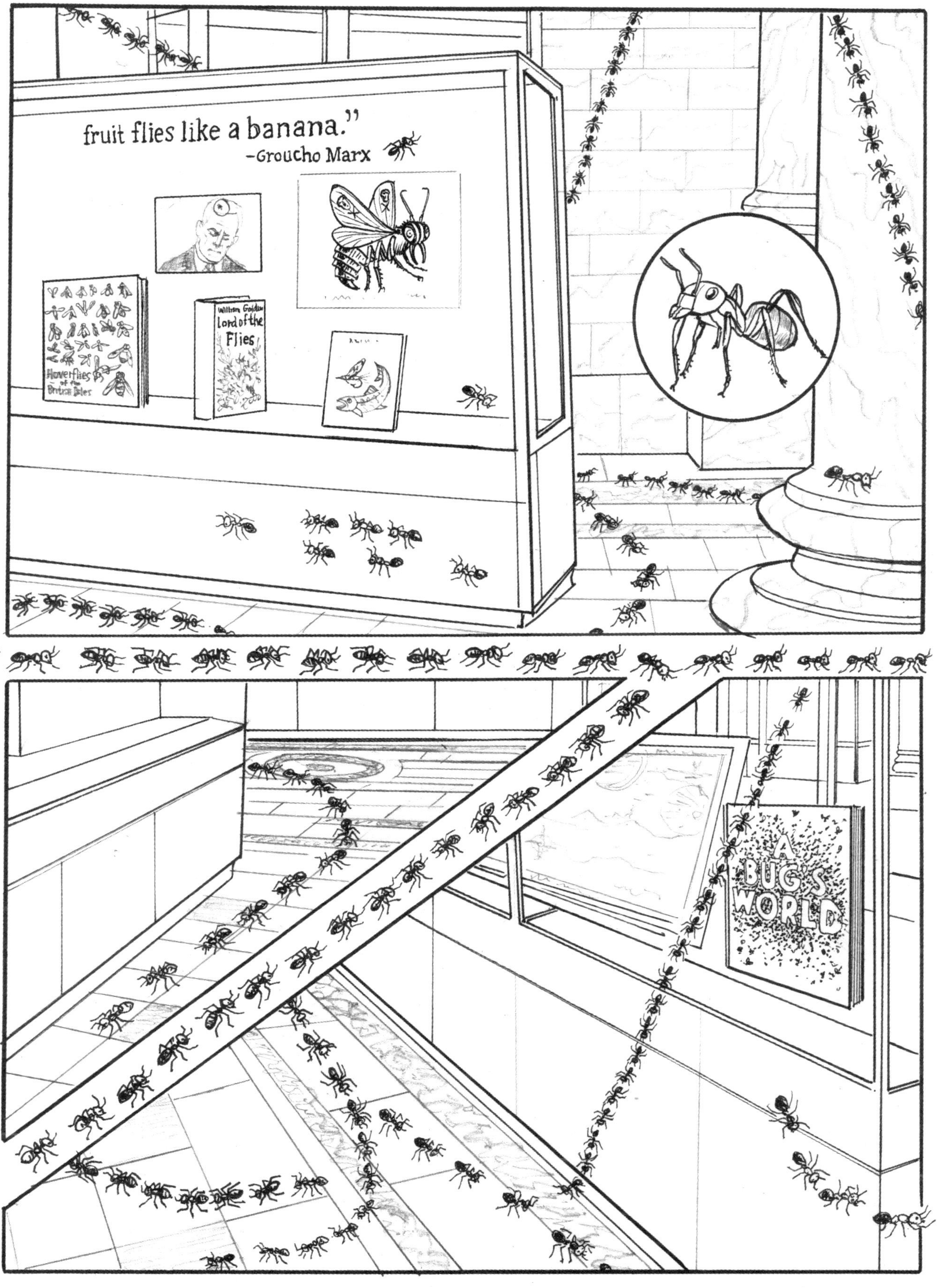
fruit flies like a banana."
-Groucho Marx
Hoverflies of the British Isles
William Golding
Lord of the Flies
A BUG'S WORLD

*"I am dying by inches
from not having
anybody to talk to
about insects."*

— Charles Darwin
(1809-1882)
from a letter written to his
second cousin, William Darwin Fox

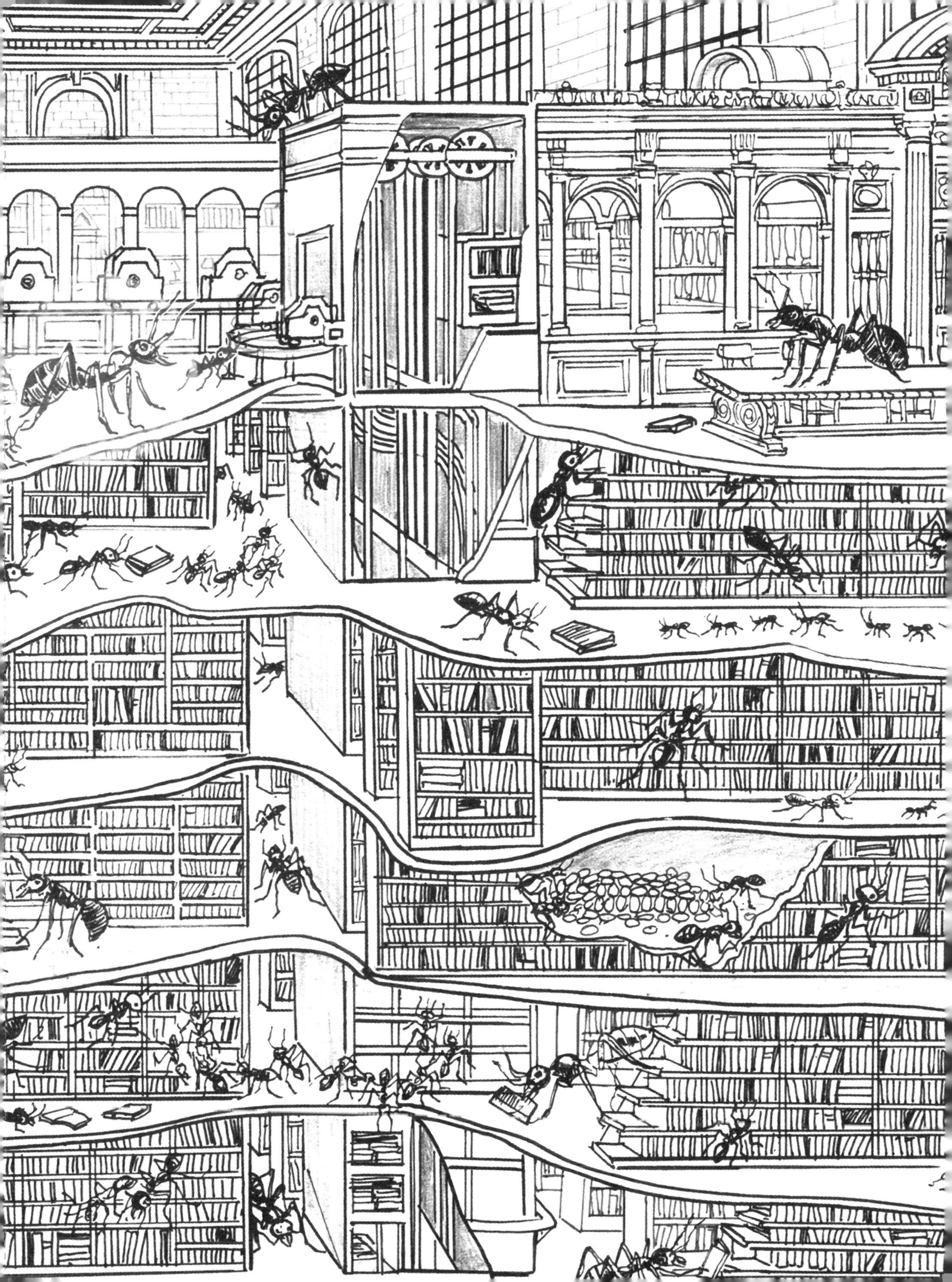

"Time is rhythm: the insect rhythm
of a warm humid night, brain ripple,
breathing, the drum in my temple—
these are our faithful timekeepers..."

—Vladimir Nabokov
(1899-1977)
from
Lectures on Literature

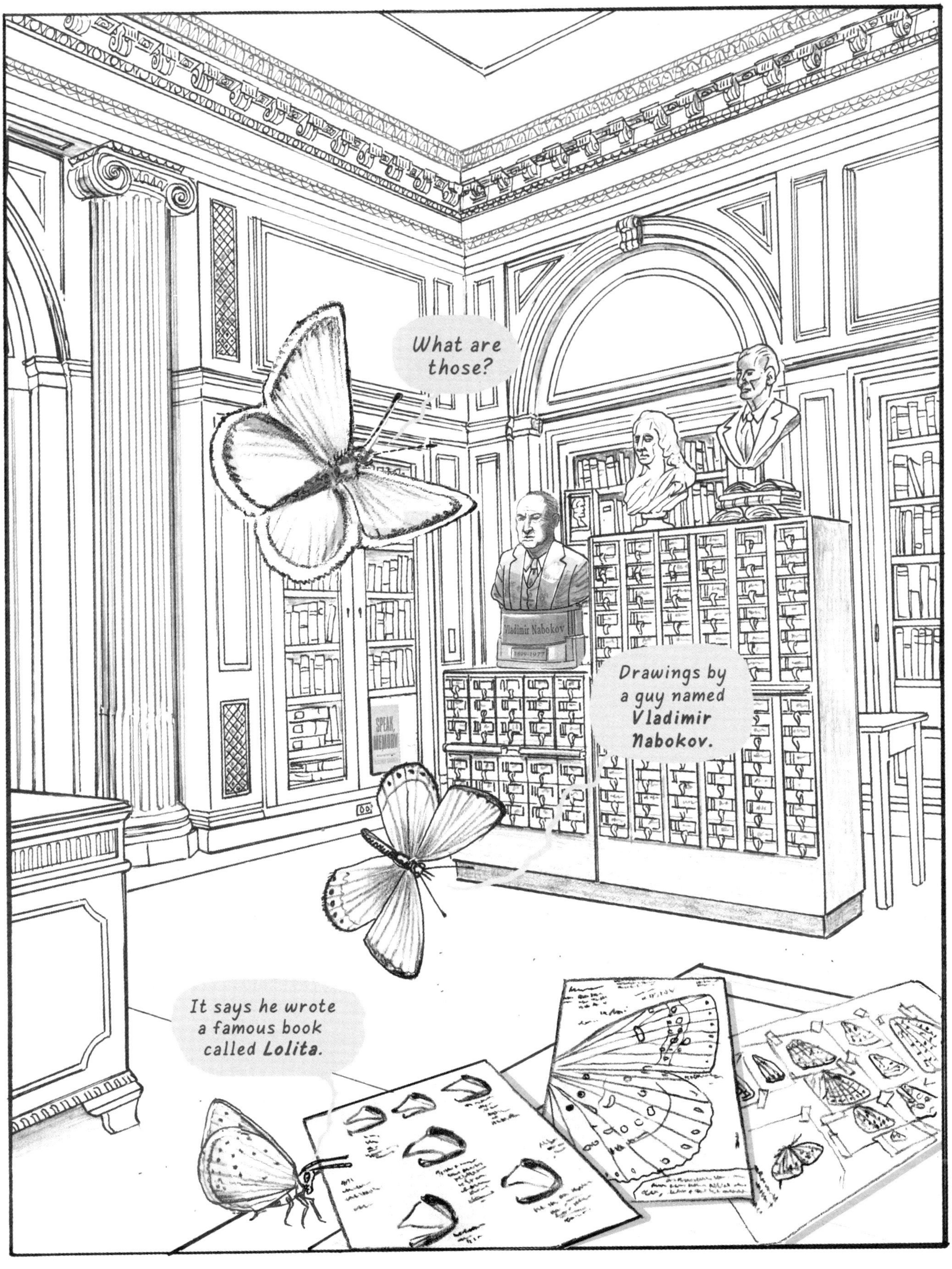
What are those?
Vladimir Nabokov
Drawings by a guy named Vladimir Nabokov.
It says he wrote a famous book called Lolita.

According to legend,
silk was discovered
in 2640 B.C.E. by a
Chinese empress
named Leizu...

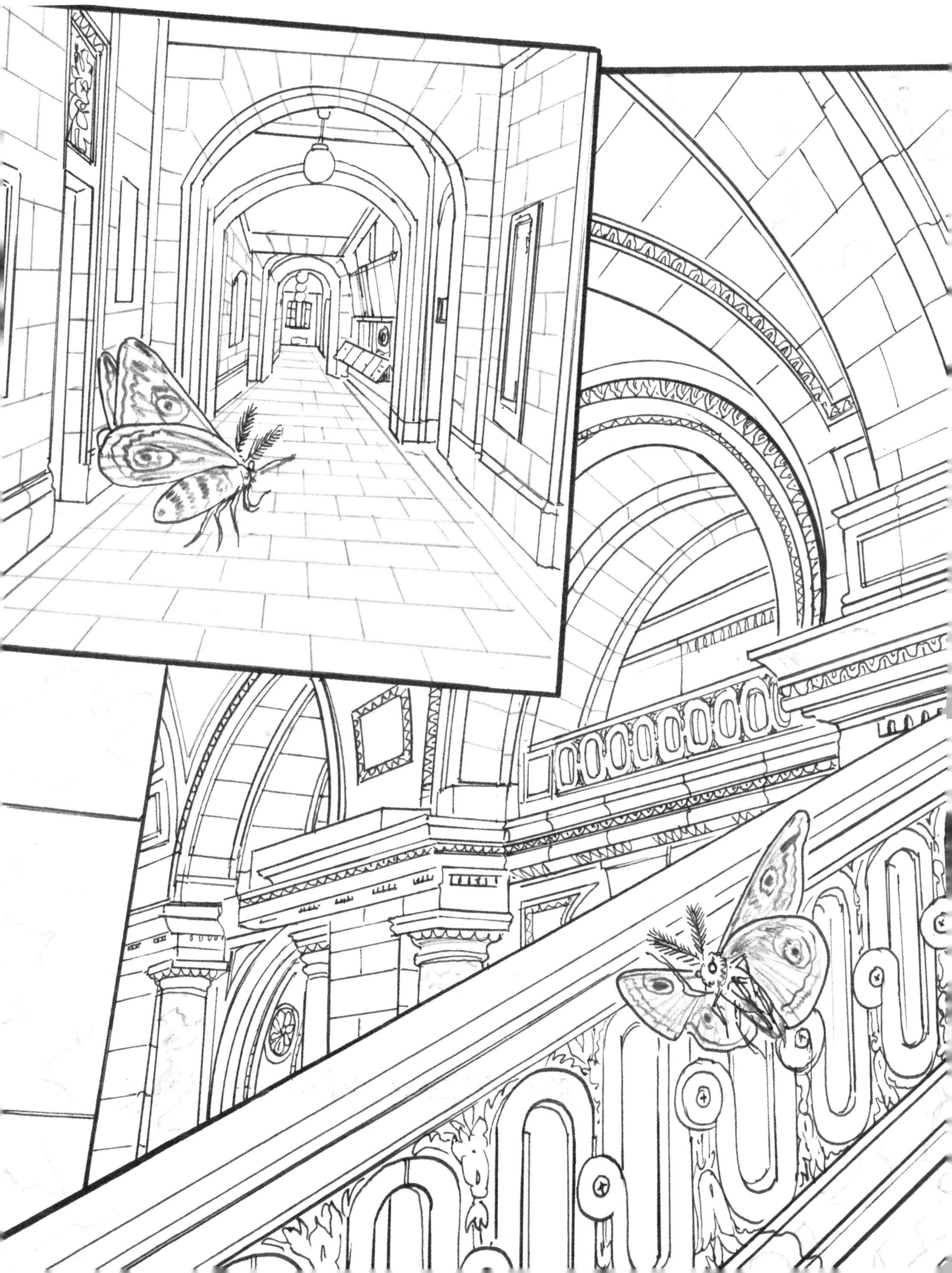

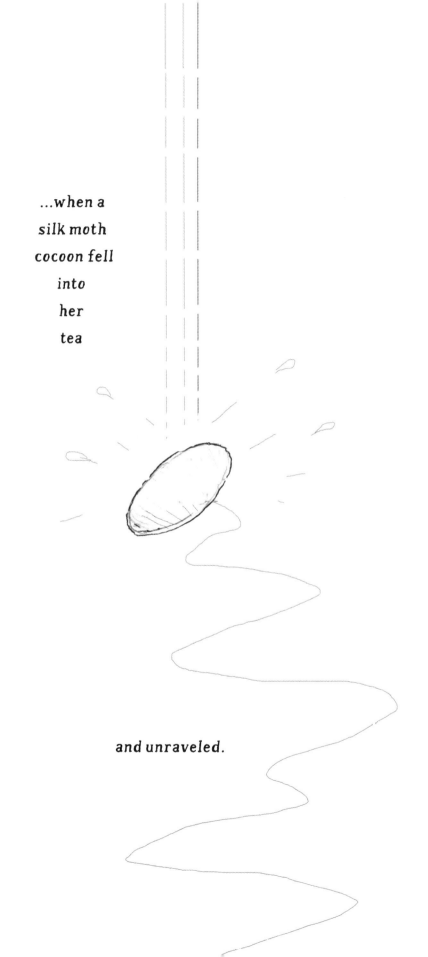

...when a
silk moth
cocoon fell
into
her
tea

and unraveled.

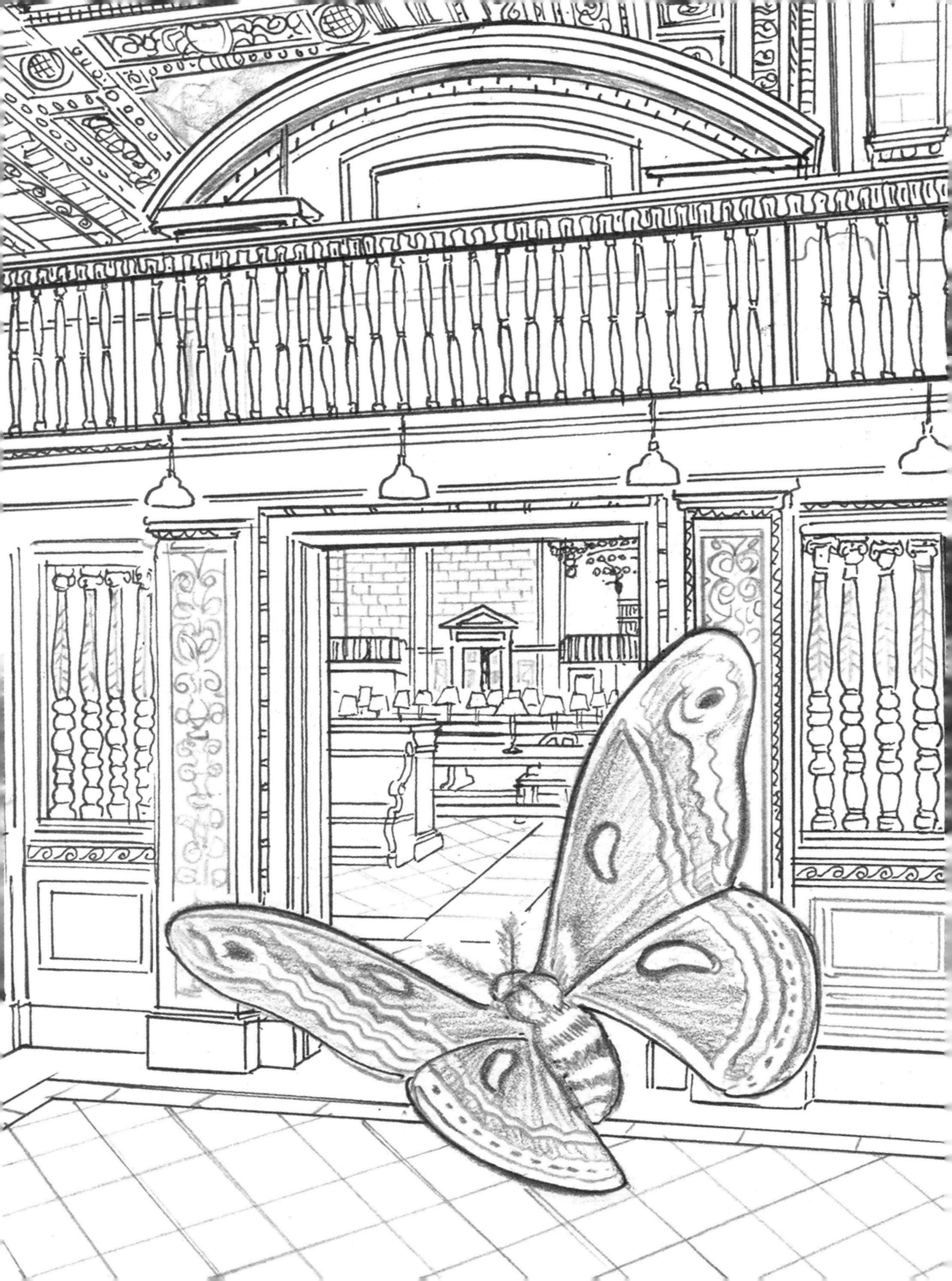

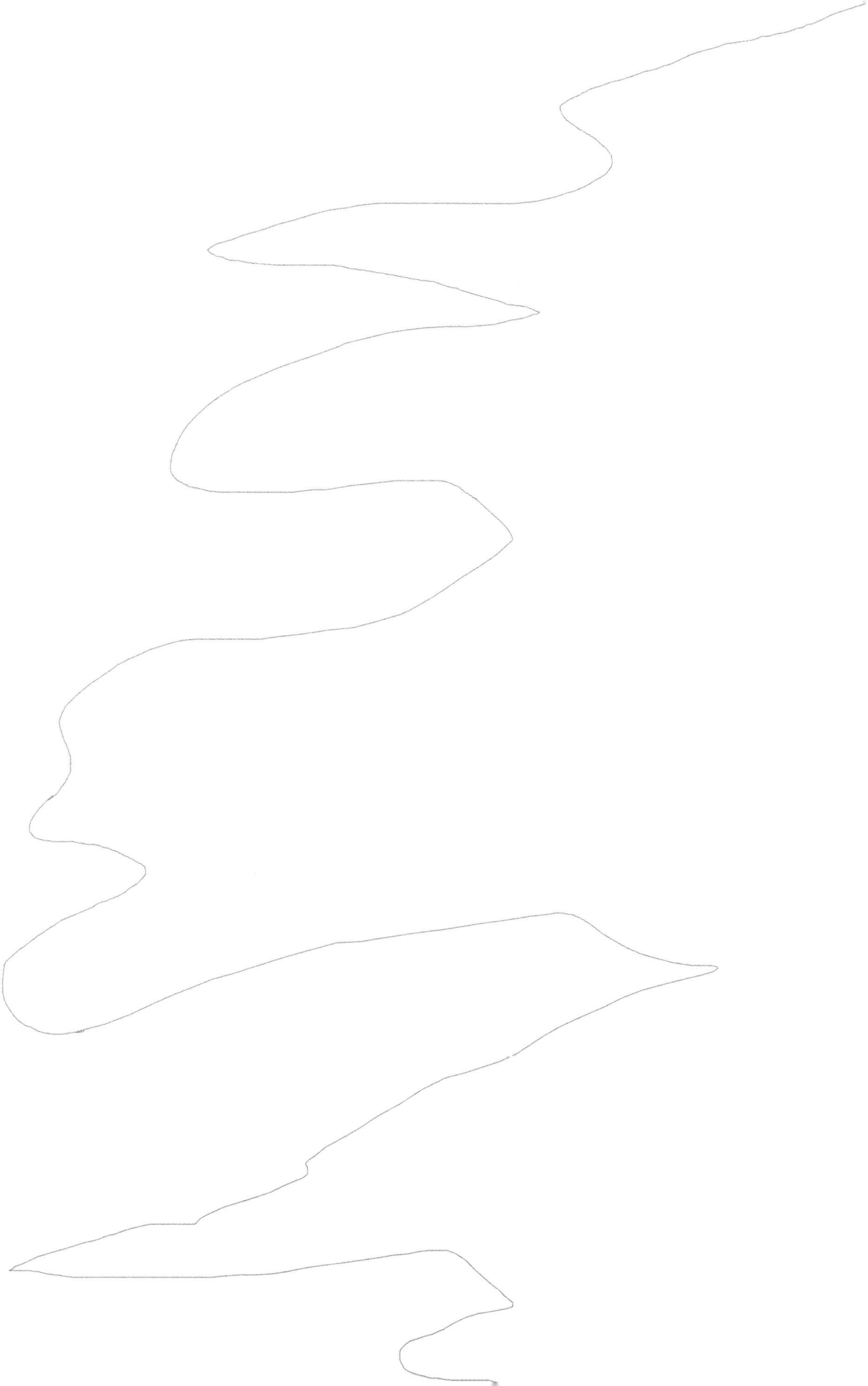

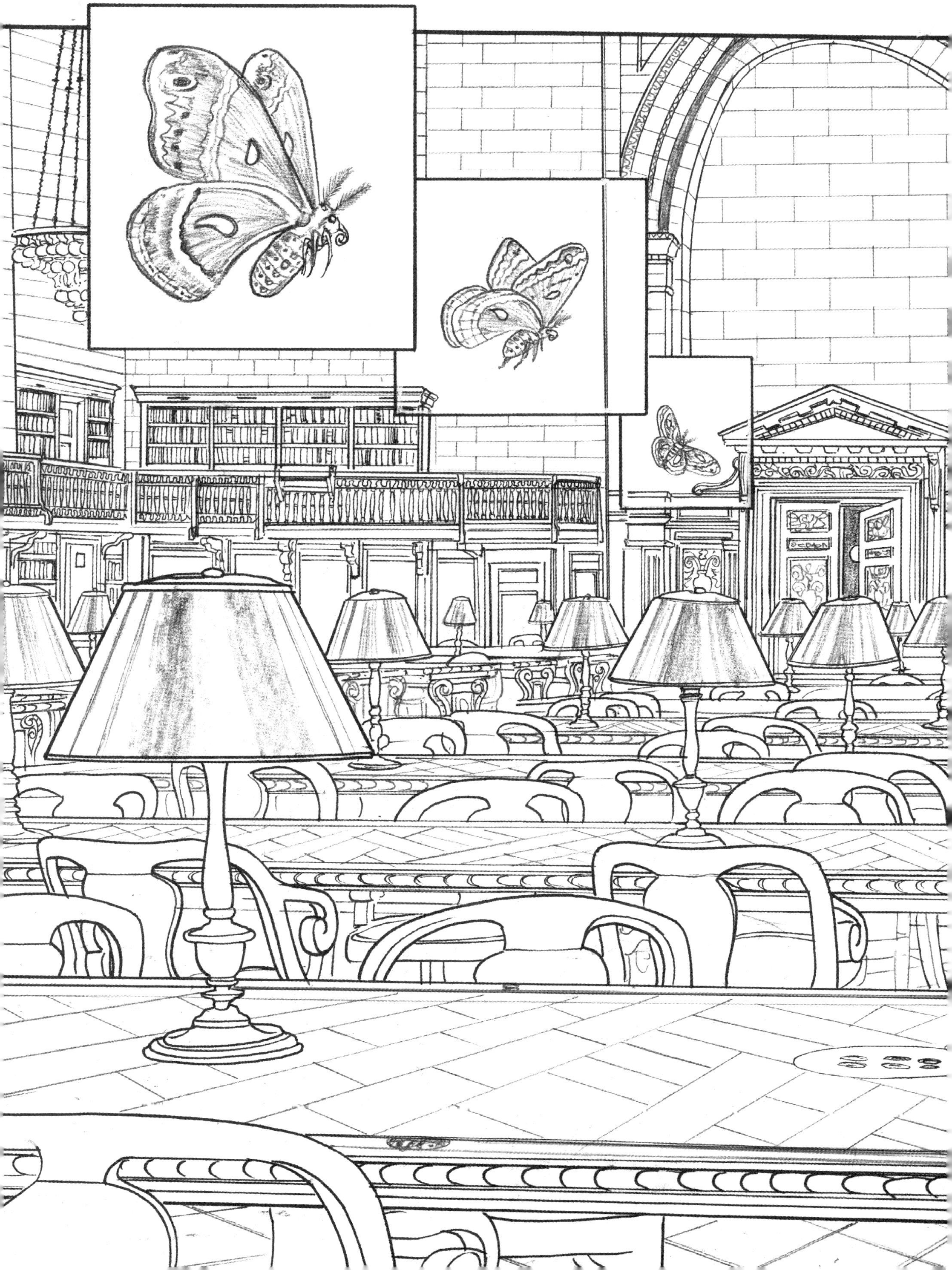

A silk moth is
able to produce
up to six inches
of thread
a minute.

The silk industry
manufactures seventy
million pounds of silk a year,
which requires nearly
ten billion cocoons.

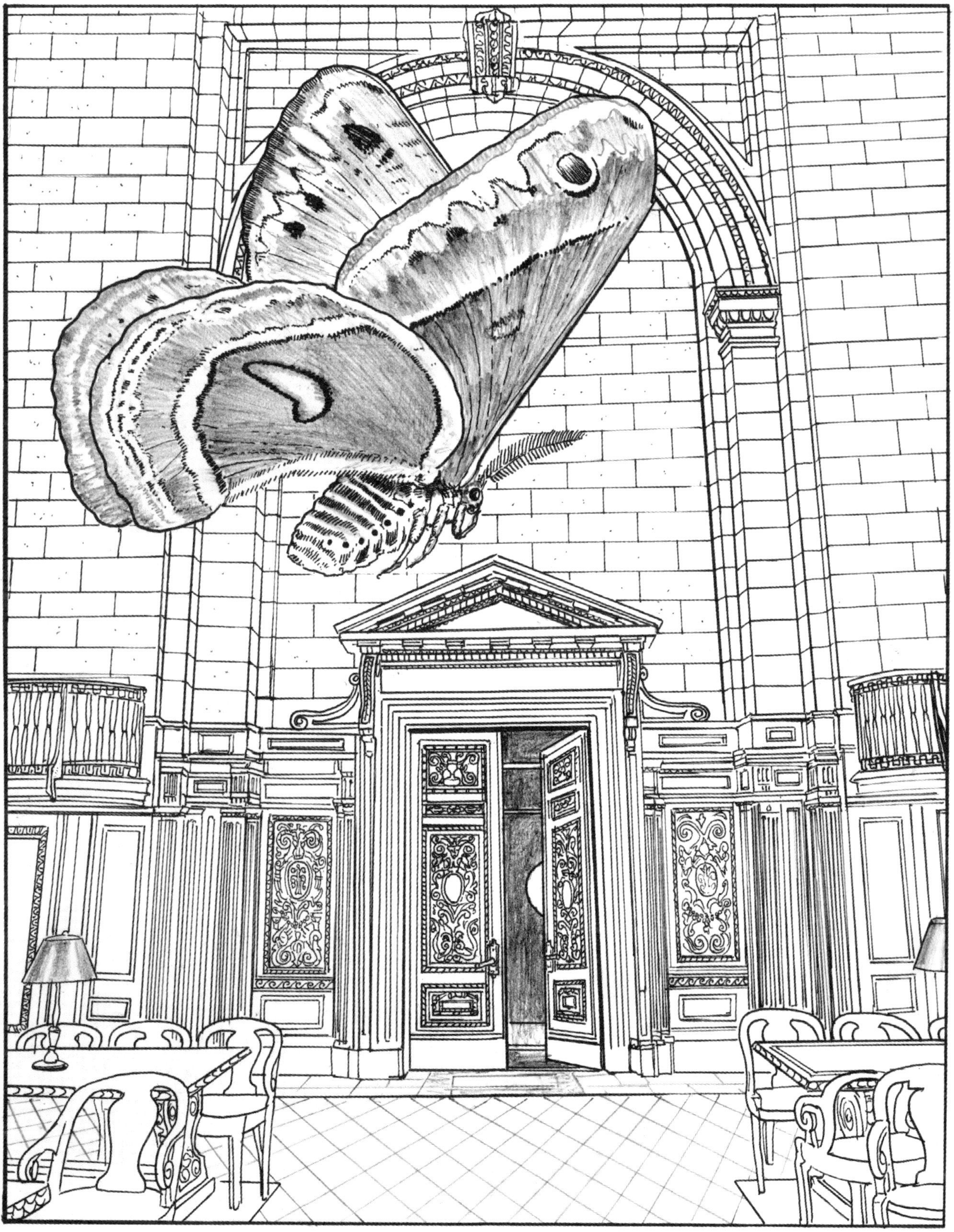

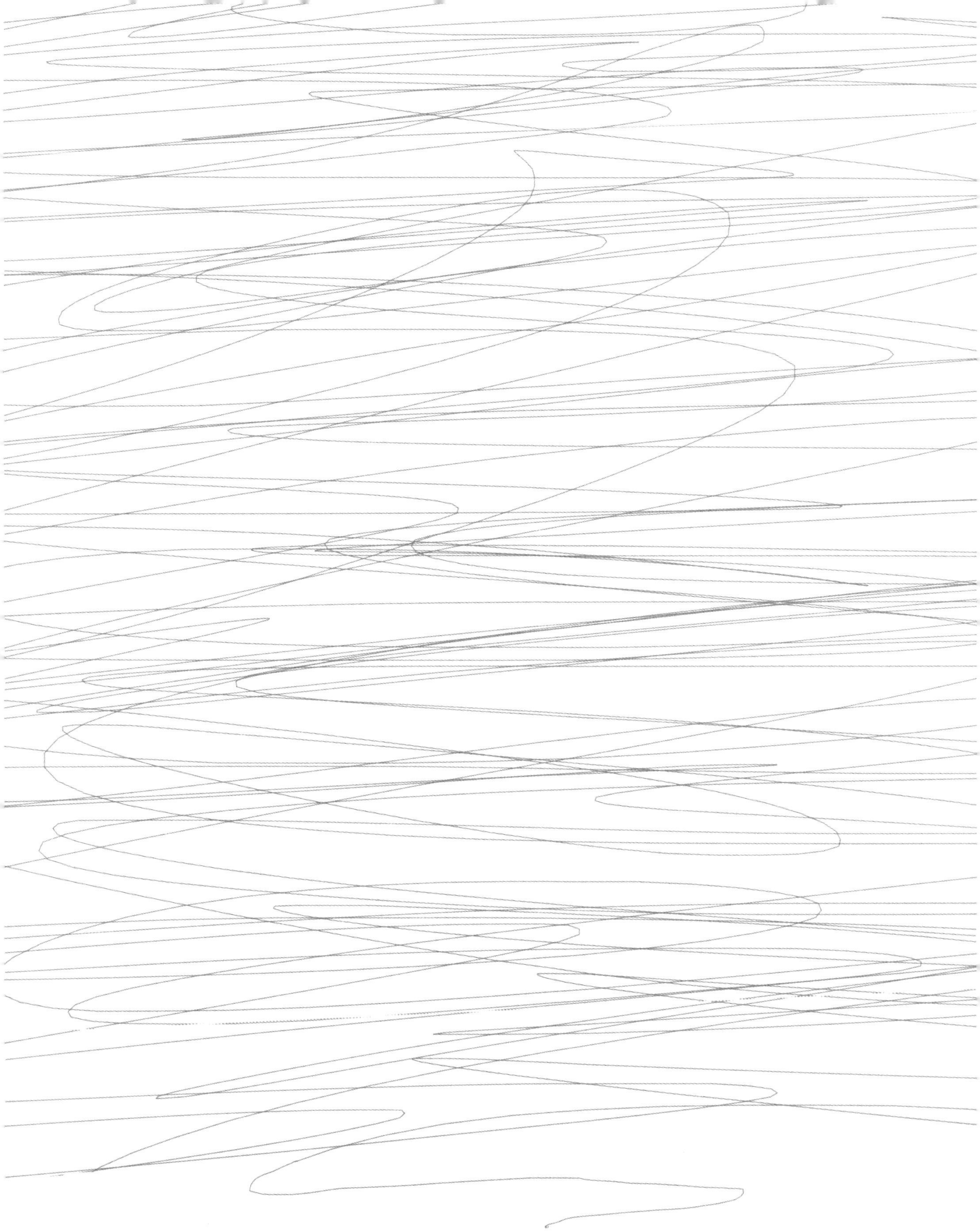

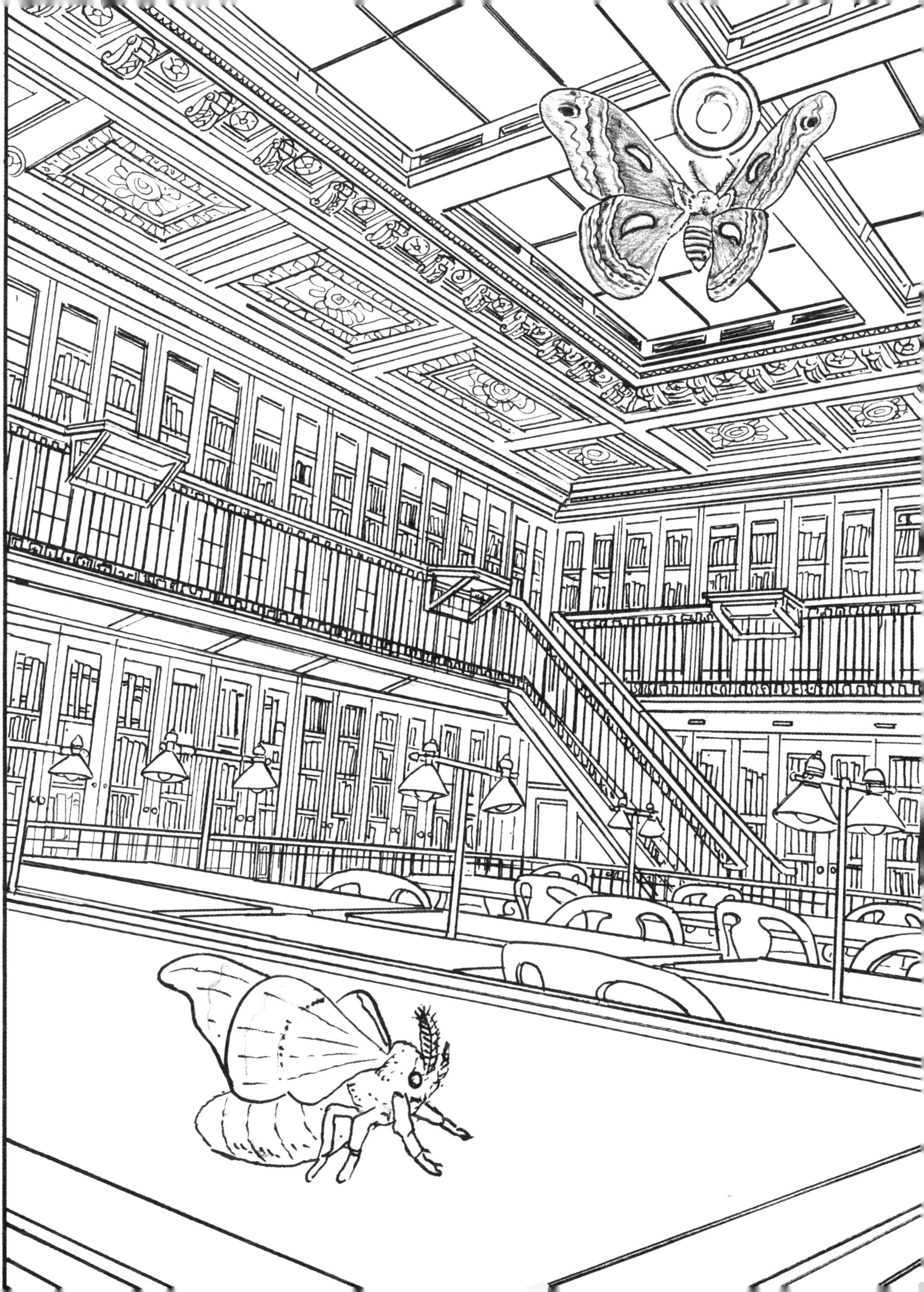

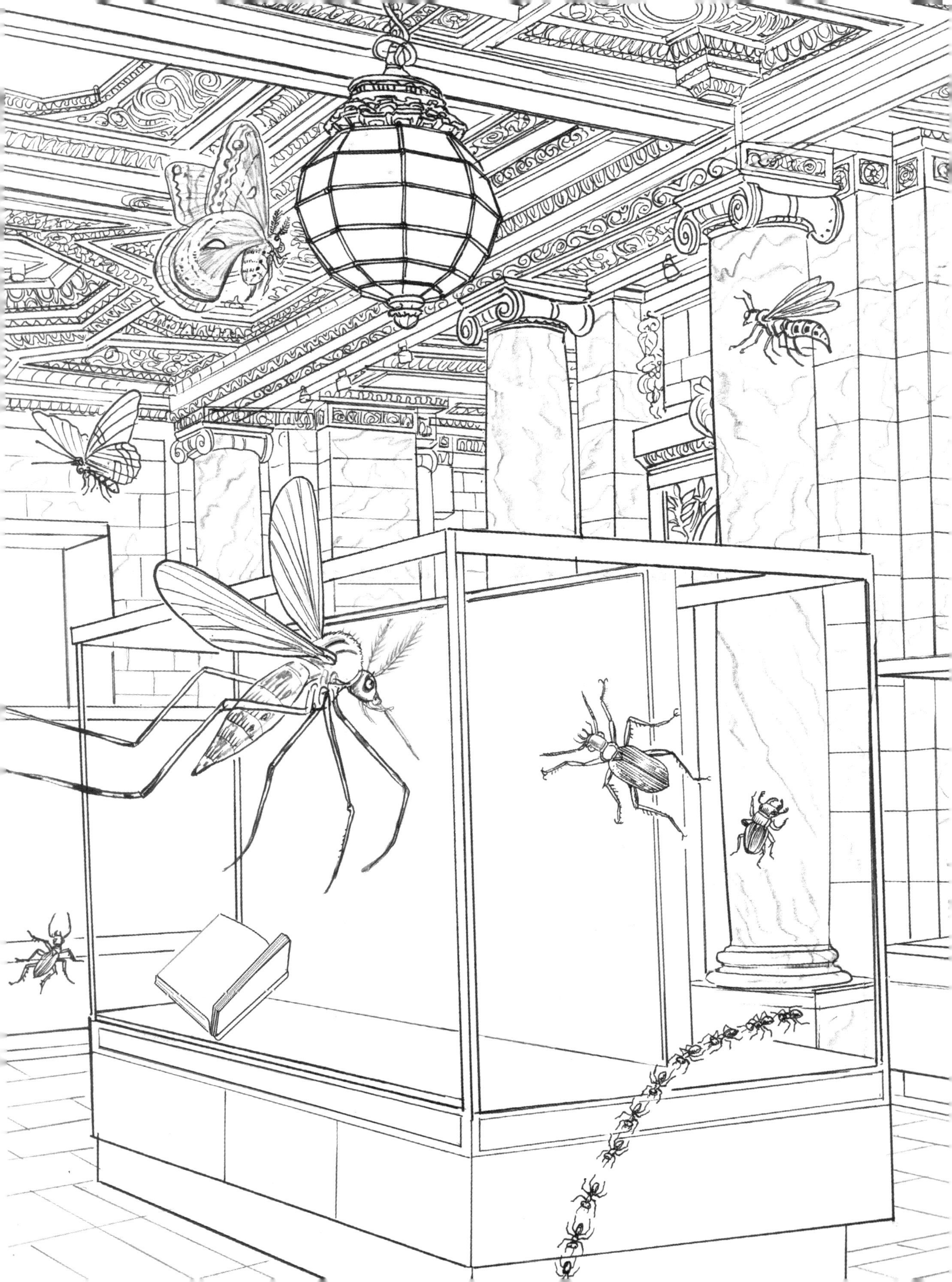

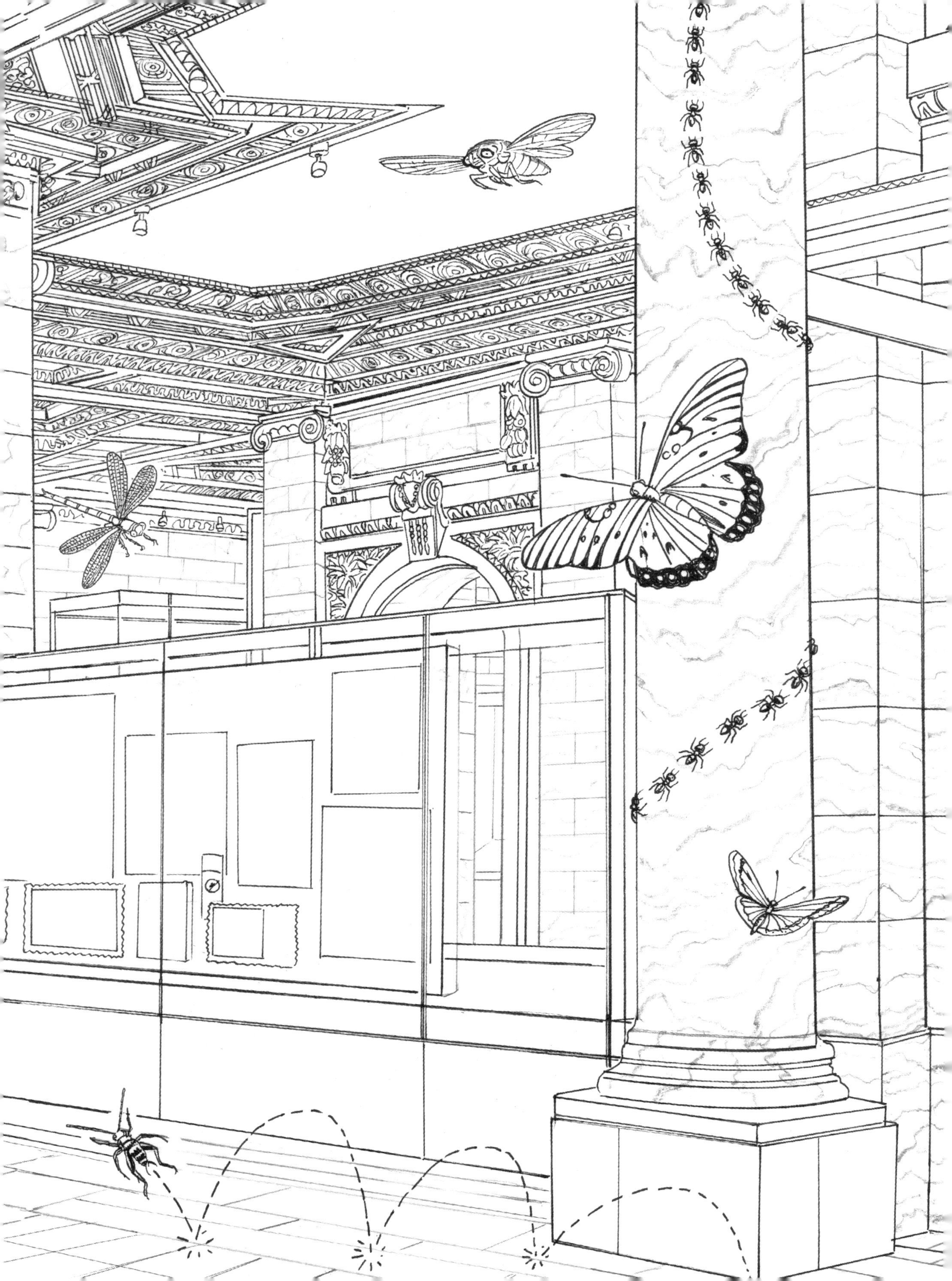

Biting midges, also
known as "no-see-ums,"
pollinate the cacao tree.

Without them, there
would be no chocolate.

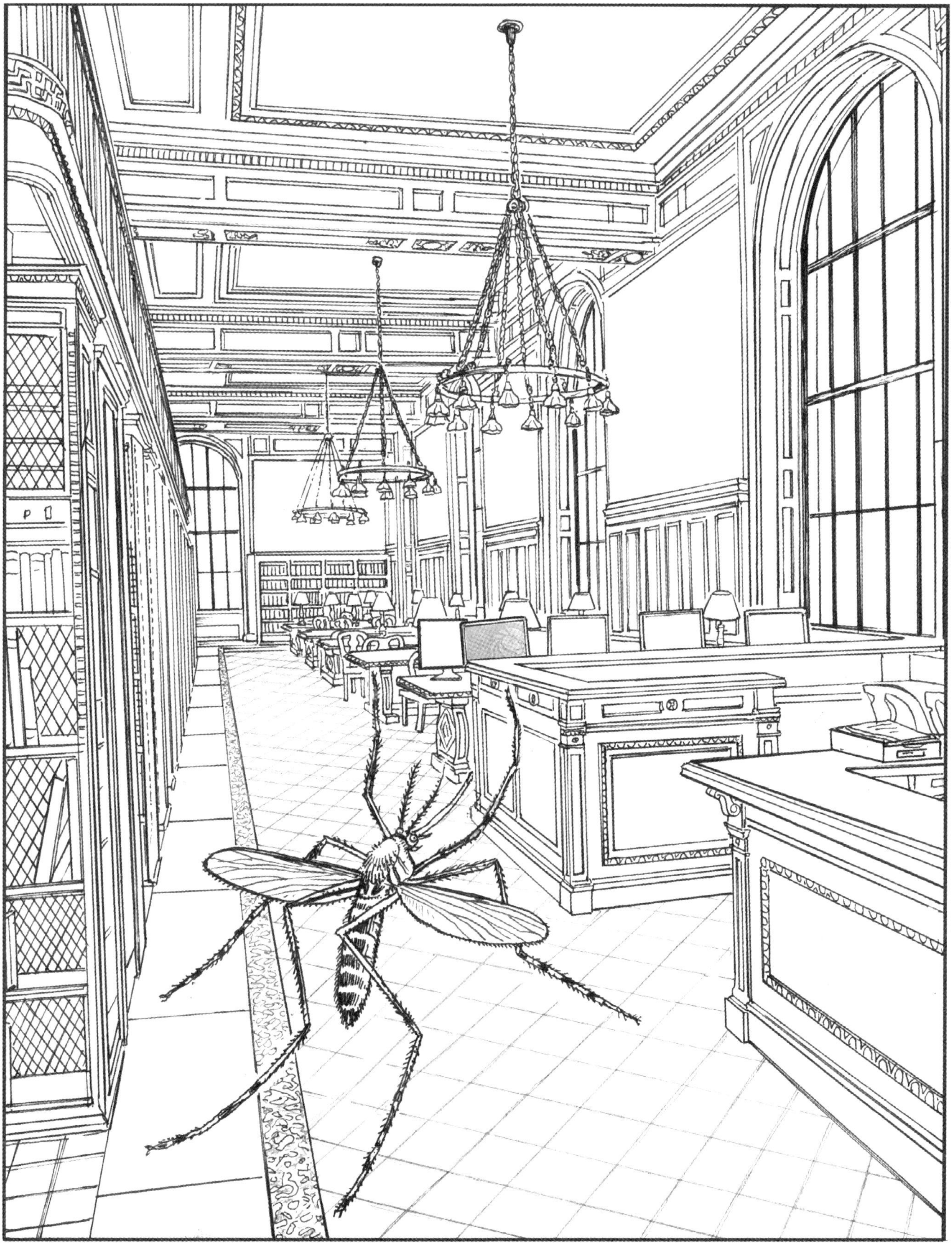

There are thousands
of mosquito species.
Contrary to popular belief,
only a few carry disease.

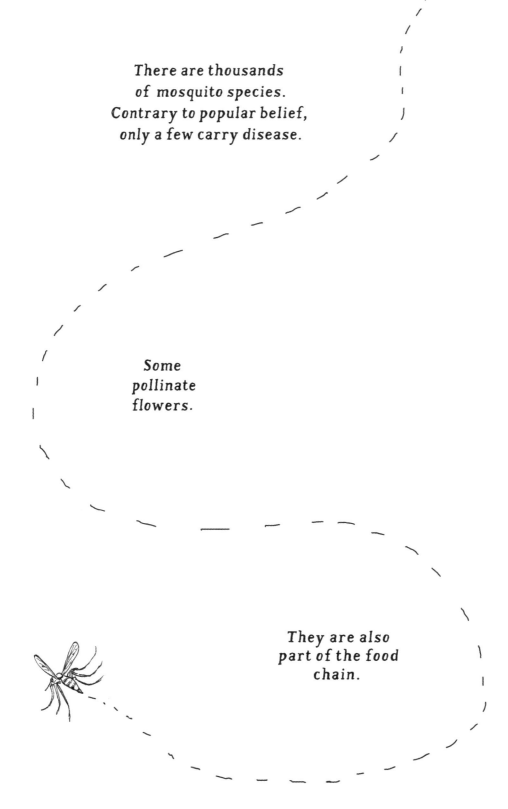

Some
pollinate
flowers.

They are also
part of the food
chain.

Birds, fish, and amphibians depend on them for nourishment.

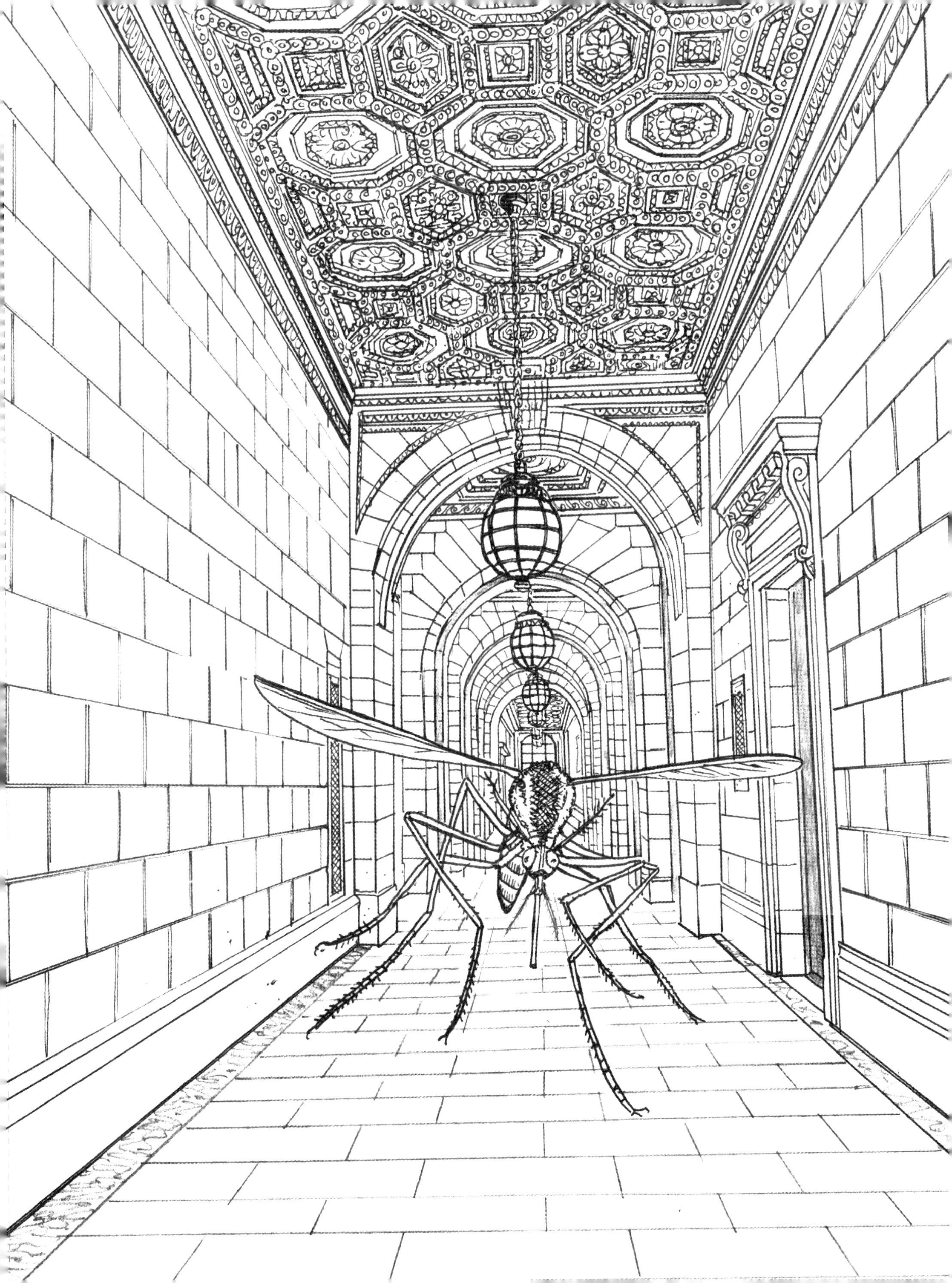

"'What sort of insects do you rejoice in,
where YOU come from?'
the Gnat inquired.

'I don't REJOICE in insects at all,'
Alice explained,
'because I'm rather afraid of them—
at least the large kinds.
But I can tell you the names of some of them.'"

—Lewis Caroll
(1832–1898)
from
*Through the Looking-Glass,
and What Alice Found There*

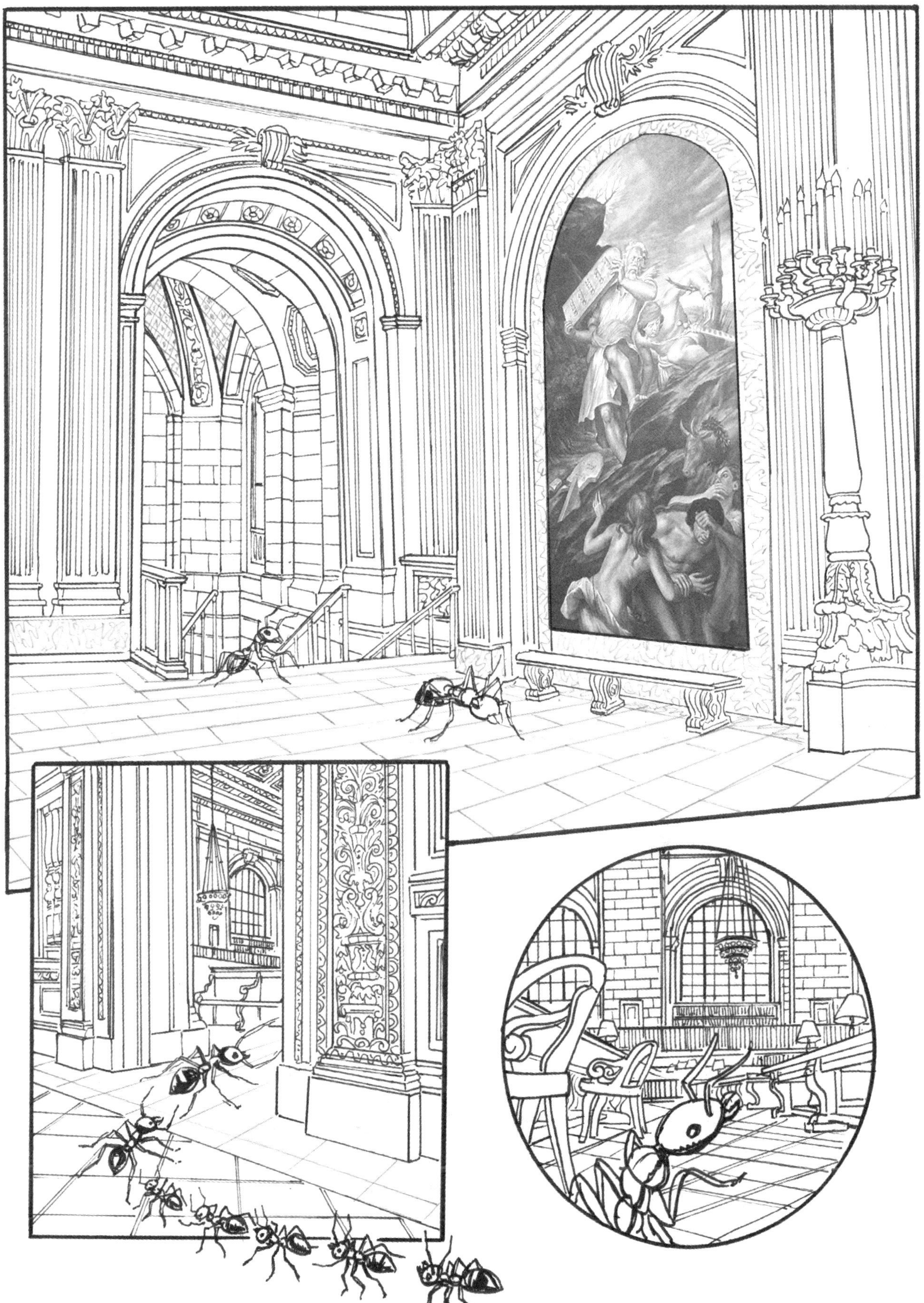

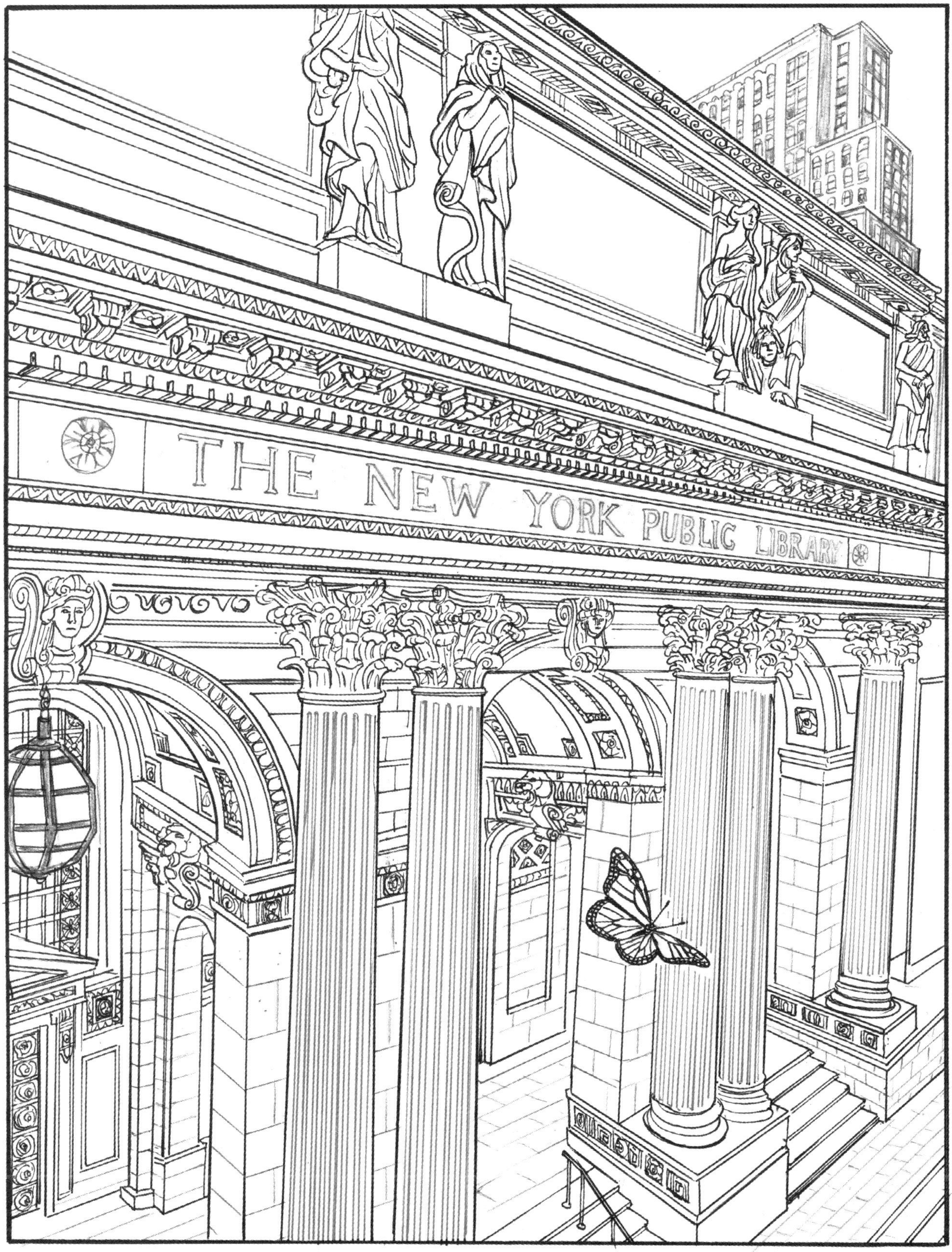
THE NEW YORK PUBLIC LIBRARY

"Everything is determined
by forces over which we have no control.
It is determined for the insect, as well as for the star.
Human beings, vegetables, or cosmic dust, we all dance
to a mysterious tune, intoned in the distance
by an invisible piper."

—Albert Einstein

(1879-1955)
from
The World As I See It

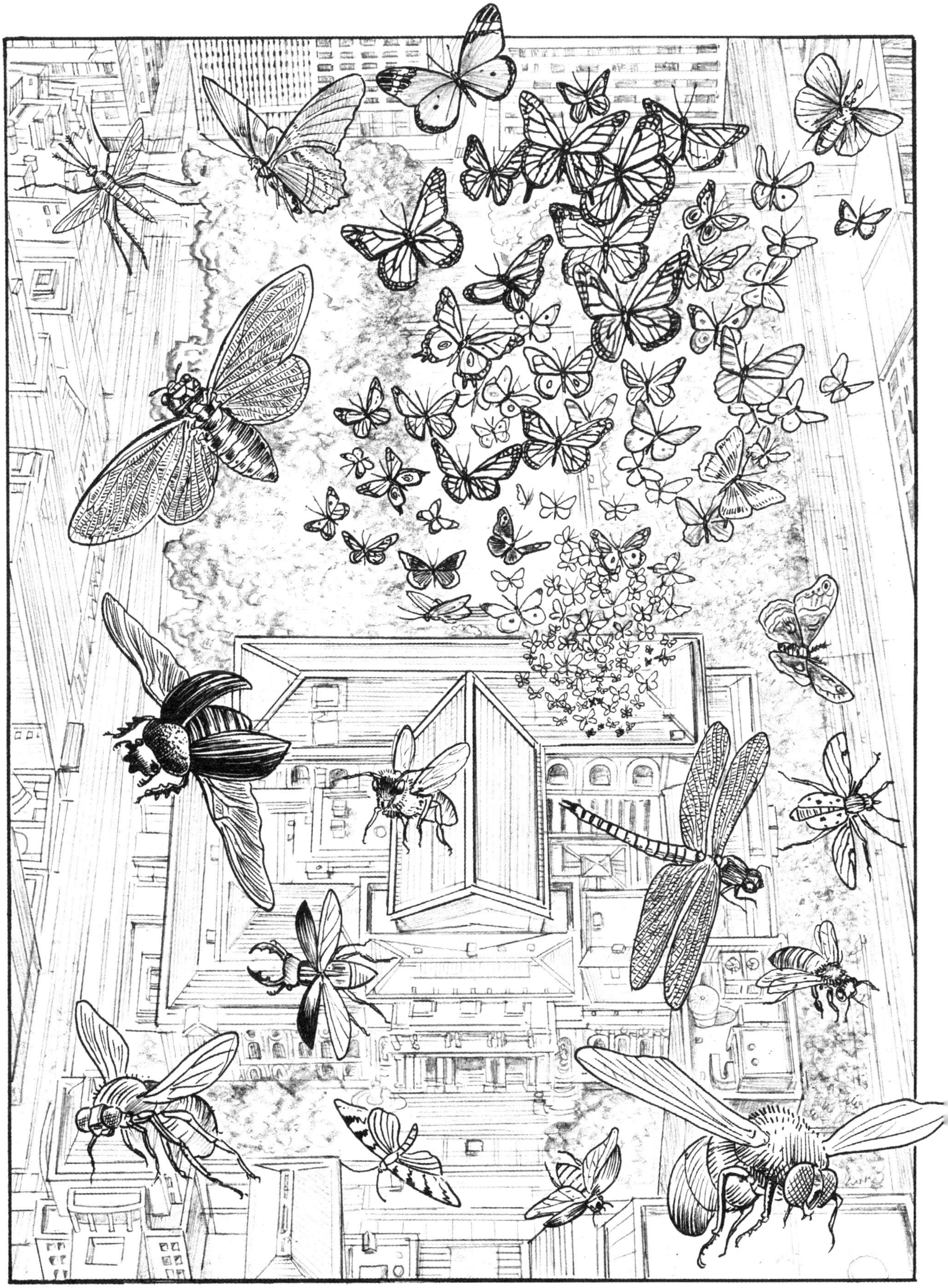

Adapted from *Insectopolis:*
A Natural History published in 2025
by W.W. Norton & Company, Inc.

Copyright © 2026, 2025 by Peter Kuper

This book's QR code–linked audio features (produced,
codirected, and cowritten by Charles Cuykendall Carter;
cowritten and codirected by Peter Kuper) originally appeared
in Peter Kuper's 2022 installation at the New York Public Library,
INterSECTS. They appear here courtesy of NYPL. Lions image
and logo © The New York Public Library. Printed with permission.

QR code soundtracks by David Rothenberg
from his album *Bug Music* © 2013 Published
by Mysterious Mountain Music (BMI).
All rights reserved. Used by permission.

All rights reserved
Printed in the United States of America

For information about permission to reproduce
selections from this book, write to Permissions,
Countryman Press, 500 Fifth Avenue, New York, NY 10110

For information about special discounts for bulk purchases,
please contact W. W. Norton Special Sales at
specialsales@wwnorton.com or 800-233-4830

Manufacturing by Versa Press
Production manager: Devon Zahn

Countryman Press
www.countrymanpress.com

An imprint of W. W. Norton & Company, Inc.
500 Fifth Avenue, New York, NY 10110
www.wwnorton.com

978-1-324-11158-0

1 2 3 4 5 6 7 8 9 0

Special thanks to:
Emily Russell
Barrett Klein
Betty Russell
Emma Peters
Ann Treistman

Also by Peter Kuper
Monarch's Flight
Insectopolis
Ruins
Diario de Oaxaca
Adaptations:
The Metamorphosis
Kafkaesque
Heart Of Darkness